Bedford Pim

**The Negro and Jamaica**

Bedford Pim

**The Negro and Jamaica**

ISBN/EAN: 9783337321383

Printed in Europe, USA, Canada, Australia, Japan

Cover: Foto ©Andreas Hilbeck / pixelio.de

More available books at **www.hansebooks.com**

# THE NEGRO

AND

# JAMAICA.

BY

COMMANDER BEDFORD PIM,

ROYAL NAVY.

READ BEFORE

THE ANTHROPOLOGICAL SOCIETY OF LONDON,

FEBRUARY 1, 1866,

AT

ST. JAMES'S HALL, LONDON.

LONDON:

TRÜBNER AND CO., 60, PATERNOSTER ROW.

1866.

# PREFACE.

WHEN the news of the Jamaica rebellion arrived in this country I felt that at last my countrymen, whether they liked it or not, were brought face to face with the negro, and that a clear view of his peculiarities should be laid before them, so as to assist in properly handling this most important subject, whether politically or religiously, in such a manner as to aid in settling the question.

The only scientific tribunal before which this could be done with effect was that vigorous and fearless body, the Anthropological Society of London, whose labours will be better appreciated when it is understood that the numerous races composing our vast empire can only be governed properly by studying their anthropological characteristics. This Society has already done good service in bringing forward the facts of "the black question," by the publication of several excellent memoirs, amongst which that of its President, Dr. James Hunt, on 'The Negro's Place in Nature,' has acquired a well-merited popularity.

My paper on 'The Negro at Home and Abroad' having been accepted by the Anthropological Society, the demand for tickets of admission was so great that it was found necessary to secure St. James's Hall, the rooms of the Society in St. Martin's Place being too small.

On the 1st of February the spacious hall was crowded with persons eager to obtain that information so studiously withheld, or so wilfully perverted by those who have hitherto attempted to lead public opinion.

The unanimous demonstration of a crowded and highly respectable audience in favour of the arguments used in my Paper, based as they were known to be on long practical experience of the Negro character, leads me to hope that I have brought forward my facts opportunely, and that the shallowness and impiety of those who have dared to compare the wretched Gordon with St. Stephen, nay even with our Saviour himself, will be, in the future, thoroughly understood.

Does England owe one particle of her proud position to the patriotism, the self-denial, or the statesmanlike teachings of the professional philanthropists of Exeter Hall ? Fearless of contradiction, I reply that the very reverse is the case.

Jealous of the honour and dignity of my country, I have felt keenly the course taken by our Government in Jamaican affairs. Whether or not they have been urged thereto by rowdy deputations, based on "eight miles of dead bodies," and other equally clever fabrications, one thing is certain, that a public servant of whom any country might be proud—" one of the very finest types of English manhood "—has been deposed and degraded for making the safety of his trust the supreme law.

Why was not the example of Governor Eyre, in his generous readiness to accept responsibilities scarcely belonging to him, and his manly determination to support his subordinates at all hazards, followed by his superiors at home,—at least *until proof had been obtained,* that the malignant assertions of his enemies had some foundation in fact ?

The weakness and short-sightedness of our present policy with regard to Jamaica, can only lead to one result, viz. that of making it impossible for the whites to live in the island with any degree of security ; a regular exodus of all the white settlers will soon become inevitable; and I do not see how to prevent the contagion from spreading all over the West Indies. Such an emigration would be to me personally most valuable, possessing as I do the control of a million and a half of acres of land in Central America, where such a body of acclimatized and enterprising people would be received with open arms, and soon prove extremely valuable in swelling its resources. But the plain duty which every Englishman owes to the land of his birth made me put aside these and similar considerations, and compelled me to point out the danger of adhering to a policy which must crush out all zeal and decision in our public servants, and which is pregnant with evil to the progress of our colonial empire all over the world.

BEDFORD PIM.

*Belsize Square, Hampstead,*
*February,* 1866.

# THE NEGRO.

## PART I.

### IN THE OLD WORLD.

I DO not propose this evening to enter into a merely technical dissertation on the subject which has been announced to you. I wish rather to show the negro's place in history, in other words, his ancient and modern condition. First, in his own country and, secondly, abroad.

Undoubtedly, at this moment the chief interest of our subject lies in recent events and the lessons which the merest review of the past and present condition of any large portion of the human race must necessarily suggest.

And here I would say at the outset, that I do not believe in the morality of palliating murder and rebellion, whether committed by a black or a white; nor do I deem it right to stand forth as the champion of the theoretical grievances of every low-caste and depraved population of our empire.

I shall therefore speak of the negro as I find him in history and in life, though in so doing I may be compelled to present him in language somewhat different from the maudlin eulogiums bestowed upon him of late by the enthusiastic negrophilists of Exeter Hall. Up to the present time it must be admitted that the *origin* of the negro is most obscure; whatever service, therefore, science may yet render in clearing up this obscurity, one thing is certain, that even yet there is little but conjecture to guide us.

B

Anthropologists,—although still far from having completed even a rudimentary study of that part of the human race of which the black man is the type,—have nevertheless succeeded in eliminating from a confused mass of opinion certain facts which may ultimately set at rest the vexed question of the *equality* of two great divisions of the human family.

Theories of origin are not wanting : one points to Cain, as the wicked progenitor of the race; another, with equal confidence, fixes upon Canaan, the son of Ham, who, the Bible tells us, went out into the world under a curse.

But with regard to such theories, it is not a little curious, as showing the inconsistencies of our professional philanthropists, that whilst they invariably and with great Scriptural unction adopt one or the other of these views, they at the same time insist on the absolute equality between a race, to which they delight to point as labouring under a curse for thousands of years, and a people which has advanced in comparatively modern times to the highest degree of civilization.

There is still another theory to which I must allude, viz. that Adam and Eve were black ;—that civilization in the course of ages whitened the skin;—and that only the refuse of society continues of the primitive colour.

These, however, can only be called guesses as to the origin of the negro, and, in a scientific point of view, they are absolutely valueless.

But let us leave the regions of doubt, and see what kind of information can be gleaned from the light of history. Here the mind naturally reverts to those imperishable monuments, so profusely scattered over the land of Egypt, and which have proved such unerring pilots to discovery. The sculptures carry us back thousands of years before the Christian era,—thousands of years before the people of this country were even known as the rudest of savages,—and on them we find the well-known features of the negro, portrayed with a fidelity and truth, which leave not a doubt of his identity,—as being, in fact, the counterpart of the African of the present day.

Nilotic antiquities, however, are not the only guides to a comparison between the negro of that early period and our own. The hieroglyphics are doubtless most valuable, as giving an idea of the manners and customs of the Egyptians, and especially as showing the position held by the negro amongst an early civi-

lized race; but in addition, we are in possession of the actual
bodies of those who thought, moved, and worked on the earth at
that distant time.

Thanks to the art of embalming, we possess the mummy-head
of a negress, showing the lineaments so perfectly, that if the
individual had been an old acquaintance we should at once
recognize her. Here we have the facial angle of 70°, the low,
compressed forehead, the flattened nose and face,—in short, all
those characteristics with which we are so familiar at the present
day. This mute testimony is the strongest confirmation of the
sculptured records, and is also proof positive that the negro of
that period was in immediate contact with a high state of civilization.

Other mummies, excavated at the same time and country,
are of a higher type; for, notwithstanding the bitumen which
has blackened the skin, the facial angle, elevation of forehead,
aristocratic nose, hair still soft and silky, prove this, and leave
no room for cavil or doubt.

We may thus, without fear of contradiction, fix the position of
the negro at the earliest period recorded in the world's history.
He was then a menial,—in other words, a slave; nay more, the
lowest type of man known to the civilization of that day.

Century after century rolls away; page after page of the hieroglyphics is unfolded; but not the smallest change is discoverable
in the condition of the negro. On the banks of the Nile, I
have myself carefully examined some of the earliest hieroglyphics in which the negro is depicted, and also some of a thousand
years later; but it would have taken the eye of a microscopist
to detect the slightest difference in any of the characteristics
of the race, although so wide an interval of time had elapsed, and
so close a connection with a higher civilization existed.

I have thus endeavoured to point out the actual status of the
negro at the period of his first appearance in history five thousand years ago, and to show that a long connection with civilization had in no way modified either his form or nature; but to
those of my countrymen who have not travelled in Egypt, and
yet desire to inform themselves more fully on this peculiar subject, I would commend the papyrus rolls at the British Museum;
as teaching somewhat more of the individual than can be gained
from the descriptions given in Exeter Hall.

I will now take another downward step on the ladder of time, and show what our more immediate predecessors in civilization, the Greeks and Romans, thought of the negro; and although it would be easy to multiply the proof that the civilization of these had no more effect on the negro than that of the Egyptian, yet I do not propose to take up your time with a disquisition on this part of my subject. In the days of Æschylus, and even 500 years before his time,—the days of Homer,—the negro was as well known as he is now, and, as regards his social place among races, perfectly defined. Virgil,* writing on this subject, brings us up to about 2000 years of our own times. He says—

> " From Afric she, the swain's sole serving-maid,
> Whose face and form alike her birth betrayed,
> With woolly locks, lips tumid, sable skin;
> Wide bosom, udders flaccid, belly thin,
> Legs slender; broad and most misshapen feet,
> Chapped into chinks, and parched with solar heat."

Virgil, in point of fact, photographs the negro of the present day through the cumulus of 2000 years; and his testimony alone would be sufficient to prove that as the race was then, so it is now. In short, after centuries of contact with the Egyptians, the Persians, the Greeks, the Carthaginians, the Romans, and the Arabians, the original characteristics stick to the negro; *he has gained no permanent good;* and I commend this fact to the negrophilists.

But our own history may now be appealed to, in further proof that the negro does not advance in the social scale. Cæsar tells us that the ancient Britons, 1900 years ago, were so savage that they were not even fit for slaves. This opinion is pregnant with instruction, especially in an anthropological point of view, as showing the great gulf between the European and Nigritian races. Like the Red Indian of the American continent, the ancient Britons could not exist under the restriction of their freedom; they were so savage, in other words so uncontrollable, that they could not be made to bow the neck to their conquerors.

Let me ask you for one moment to picture to yourselves the stately form of Caractacus in the streets of Rome, and his brother-slave, the negro, a prince of Ashantee we will suppose, in chains beside him, both savage, both untutored; but, in other respects, how widely different! Can any man in his senses call

* Virgil *in Moretum.*

them equals, except in affliction? Can any sane man reflect upon the nobleness of the one and the abject nature of the other, and accept the theory of equality? And if this holds good in the primitive state of the Briton, what must the intelligence of the nineteenth century think of such a comparison now?—The highest order of intellect the world has yet seen, on a level with one of the lowest! It were well to consign such a paradox to the limbo of other utopian ideas with the least possible delay.

Let us now examine the state of civilization which exists in the interior of Africa, where at all events the native is more or less free from those external influences which, as our negrophilists insist, only tend to injure his morals; and then let us see what contact with the civilization of modern Europe has done for the transplanted negro since Las Casas conceived the benevolent idea of substituting him for the rapidly disappearing aborigines of America.

With regard to the state and condition of the people of the interior of Africa, we have the most abundant testimony from all sorts of eye-witnesses. Numbers of educated men have devoted their lives to explore and describe the people and country, and from the time of Vasco da Gama to our own, modern civilization has been as much in contact with Africa as the ancient.

Travellers have explored the interior, sailors the coast-line, men of business have had practical dealings with the natives, but there is only one opinion as to the innate cruelty of the negro, his sensuality, his brutality under the influence of superstition or when excited or misled, his inbred sloth,—in short, the almost total absence of those attributes which enable other races of mankind to advance in civilization.

In 1795-6 we have Park's travels; and the experience of the eighteenth century is thus cleverly epitomized in the following extract:—"Vices the most notorious seem to be the portion of this unhappy race,—idleness, treachery, revenge, cruelty, impudence, stealing, lying, profanity, debauchery, and intemperance, are said to have extinguished the principles of natural law, and to have silenced the reproofs of conscience. They are strangers to every sentiment of compassion, and are an awful example of the corruption of man when left to himself." ('Encyclopædia Britannica,' art. Negro, 1797.)

Again, we have in 1816, the settlement at the mouth of the Gambia; in 1822, Denham and Clapperton; in 1826, Major

Laing; in 1831, the Landers; in 1841, a naval expedition of three steamers; and within the last few years the experience of Burton, Baker, Speke and Grant, Livingstone,—in short, a mass of material upon which to form a correct opinion.

To quote from all these will be unnecessary. I prefer to come to a period within the recollection of the youngest among us, in order to show that the negro of the present day is essentially the negro of the past. What does Speke say?—"Laziness is inherent in the negroes; they will not work unless compelled to do so. Having no God, in the Christian sense of the term, to fear or worship, they have no love for truth, honour, or honesty. Controlled by no government, nor yet by home ties, they have no reason to think of, or look to, the future." And he adds, after speaking of the negro tasting the sweets of liberty on board ship as a sailor, that, "If chance bring him back again to Zanzibar, he calls his old Arab master his father, and goes into slavery with as much zest as ever."

Baker, recently returned from the sources of the Nile, fully endorses Speke's opinion, and Burton, without doubt the most accomplished traveller of this century, in his 'Mission to the King of Dahome,' vol. ii. chap. xix., gives his valuable experience in the most unqualified terms :—

"My opinions have been formed mostly by comparing, after ten years of travel, 'on and off,' the Africans with the Western Asiatics, amongst whom I have lived eight years, for the most part like one of themselves.

"Touching the African, it may be observed that there are in England at least two distinct creeds :—1. That of those who know him. 2. That of those who do not. This may be predicated of most other moot-points in the negro's case; however, the singularity is, that ignorance, not knowledge,—sentimentality, not sense,—sway the practical public mind.

"One of the principal negro-characteristics is his truly savage want of veneration for God or man; hence the expressions which we should deem blasphemous in his wild state, and the peculiar tone of his prayer, commanding rather than supplicating, which distinguish him in his semi-civilization.

"He has never grasped the ideas of a personal Deity, a duty in life, a moral code, or a shame of lying.

"The negro will obey a white man more readily than a mulatto, and a mulatto rather than one of his own colour. He never thinks of claiming equality with the Aryan race, except when taught. At Whydah the French missionaries remark that their scholars always translate 'white' and 'black' by 'master' and 'slave.'

"The negro, as a rule, despises agriculture, so highly venerated by the Asiatics, Chaldæans, Chinese, Israelites, and Persians, and recognized since the days of Aristotle as the most important of all sciences.

"His highest ambition is to be a petty trader, whilst his thick skull, broad bones, and cold porous leathery skin, point him out as a born 'hewer of wood and drawer of water.'

"The cruelty of the negro is like that of a schoolboy, the blind impulse of rage, combined with want of sympathy. Thus he thoughtlessly tortures and slays his prisoners, as the youth of England torment and kill cats. He fails in the domestication of the lower animals, because he is deficient in forbearance with them.

"The negro has never invented an alphabet, a musical scale, or any other element of knowledge. Music and dancing, his passions, are, as arts, still in embryo. In the mass he will not improve beyond a certain point, and that not respectable ; he mentally remains a child, and is never capable of a generalization.

"The negro is nowhere worse than at home, where he is a curious mixture of cowardice and ferocity. With the barbarous dread and horror of death, he delights in the torments and the destruction of others, and, with more than the usual savage timidity, his highest boast is that of heroism. He is nought but self ; he lacks even the rude virtue of hospitality, and ever, as Commander Forbes has it, he 'baits with a sprat to catch a mackerel.'

"The negro, in his wild state, makes his wives work ; he will not, or rather he cannot labour, except by individual compulsion, . as in the Confederate States, or by necessity, as in Barbadoes. When so compelled, he labours well, and he becomes civilized and humanized to the extent of his small powers. When not compelled, as Sierra Leone and Jamaica prove, he becomes degraded, debauched, and depraved.

"I conclude therefore, with Franklin, the philosopher, that the negro is still as he has been for the last 4000 years, best when 'held to labour' by better and wiser men than himself.

"The removal of the negro from Africa is like sending a boy to school,—it is his only chance of improvement, of learning that there is something more in life than drumming and dancing, talking and singing, drinking and killing. After a time, colonists, returned to Africa, may exert upon the continent an effect for which we have as yet vainly looked."

Another eye-witness, Captain Canot, in a work not much known in this country, and published by Appleton and Co., of New York, in 1854, says:—"During my first visit to Digby, I promised my trading friends that I would either return to their settlement, or at least send merchandise and a clerk to establish a factory."

There were two towns at Digby governed by cousins, and this mercantile venture gave rise to a feud between them which ended in a war, in which Captain Canot himself, though not siding with either party, was taken prisoner. After describing the battle, he says:—"A palaver-house immediately in front of my quarters was the general rendezvous, and scarcely a bushman appeared without the body of some maimed and bleeding victim. The mangled but living captives were tumbled on a heap in the centre, and soon every avenue to the square was crowded with exulting savages. Rum was brought forth in abundance for the chiefs. Presently, slowly approaching from a distance, I heard the drums, horns, and war-bells, and in less than fifteen minutes, a procession of women, whose naked limbs were smeared with chalk and ochre, poured into the palaver-house to join the beastly rites. Each of these devils was armed with a knife, and bore in her hand some cannibal trophy. The wife of Jen-Ken (the leader of one party), a corpulent wretch of forty-five, dragged along the ground, by a single limb, the slimy corpse of an infant ripped alive from its mother's womb. As her eyes met those of her husband, the two fiends yelled forth a shout of mutual joy, while the lifeless babe was tossed in the air, and caught, as it descended, upon the point of a spear. Then came the *refreshment*, in the shape of rum, powder, and blood, which was quaffed by the brutes till they reeled off, with linked hands, in a wild dance around the pile of victims. As the women leaped and sang, the men applauded and encouraged. Soon the ring was broken, and with a yell each female leaped on the body of a wounded prisoner, and commenced the final sacrifice with the mockery of lascivious embraces.

"In my wanderings in African forests, I have often seen the *tiger pounce* upon its prey, and, with instinctive thirst, satiate its appetite for blood, and abandon the drained corpse; but these African negresses were neither as decent nor as merciful as the beast of the wilderness. Their malignant pleasure seemed to consist in the invention of tortures that would agonize but not slay. There was a devilish spell in the tragic scene that fascinated my eyes to the spot. A slow, lingering, tormenting mutilation was practised on the living as well as on the dead, and in every instance the brutality of the women exceeded that of the men. I cannot picture the hellish joy with which they passed from body to body, digging out eyes, wrenching off lips, tearing the ears, and slicing the flesh from the quivering bones; while the queen of the harpies crept amid the butchery, gathering the brains from each skull as a *bonne bouche* for the approaching feast." (Ch. lxi. p. 382–6.)

And lastly, I will give the opinion of an anti-slavery man, who has served many years on the Coast of Africa:—" The African has never reached, in fact, until the settlement of Liberia, a higher rank than a king of Dahomey, or the inventor of the last fashionable grisgris to prevent the devil from stealing sugarplums. No philosopher among them has caught sight of the mysteries of nature; no poet has illustrated heaven, or earth, or the life of man; no statesman has done anything to enlighten or brighten the links of human policy. In fact, if all that negroes of all generations have ever done were to be obliterated from recollection for ever, the world would lose no great truth, no profitable art, no exemplary form of life. The loss of all that is African would offer no memorable deduction from anything but the earth's black catalogue of crimes. Africa is guilty of the slavery under which she suffered; for her people made it, as well as suffered it." ('Africa, and the American Flag;' by Commander A. H. Foote, U. S. Navy, 1854, p. 207.)

Having thus given the experience of eye-witnesses on the barbarism of the negro, let us now see what some of the deepest thinkers and most profound writers have to say. An observation of Gibbon appears decisive on the subject:—" The inaction of the negroes does not seem to be the effect either of their virtue or of their pusillanimity. They indulge, like the rest of mankind, their passions and appetites, and the adjacent tribes are engaged in frequent acts of hostility. But their rude ignorance has never invented any effectual weapons; they appear incapable of forming any extensive plan of government or conquest, and the obvious inferiority of their mental faculties has been discovered and abused by the nations of the temperate zone."

The historian Alison says:—"It is impossible to arrive at any other conclusion but that, in the qualities requisite to create and perpetuate civilization, the African is decidedly inferior to the European race; and if any doubt could exist on this subject, it would be removed by the subsequent history and present state of the Haytian Republic." (Vol. ii. p. 251.)

Another writer, Professor Bledsoe, a distinguished American philosopher, speaking of the present state of the African, says:— "The native African could not be degraded. Of the 50,000,000 of inhabitants of the continent of Africa, it is estimated that 40,000,000 are slaves. The master has the power of life and death; and, in fact, his slaves are often fed, and killed, and eaten, just as we do with oxen and sheep in this country. Nay, the hind and fore quarters of men, women, and children, might there be seen hung on the shambles, and exposed for sale! Their women are beasts of burden; and when young, they are regarded as a delicacy by the palate of their pampered masters. A warrior will sometimes take a score of young females along with him, in order to enrich his feasts, and regale his appetite. As to his religion, it is even worse than his morals; or rather, his religion is a mass of disgusting immoralities. His notion of a God, and the obscene acts by which that notion is worshipped, are too shocking to be mentioned." ('Liberty and Slavery,' p. 293.)

This survey of the manners and customs of the natives of Africa would not be complete without allusion to the labours of Livingstone, who has added so largely to our knowledge of the interior of Africa; but his sentiments are undoubtedly traceable to the peculiarity of his early training as a missionary; and the influence of those amiable but one-sided men, to whom he had to look for support, has warped his better judgment. The following extract, however, from a review of Livingstone's Recent Expedition, in the 'Times' of the 12th January of this year, deals with the question in the proper spirit.

"This volume contains a minute estimate of the characteristics of these different people, and of their capacity for improvement, which, as might have been expected from the authors, is, in our judgment, somewhat too favourable. It may well be that a philanthropic observer has been able to find in these races expressions of thought, and even customs which, favourably interpreted, have something in common with a pure faith and a true morality; and we may believe that the savage virtues, implicit obedience to a chief, a kind of simple devotion in conduct, a tendency to respect superiors, generosity, and enduring patience, appear among the natives of these countries. But, hitherto, experience has shown how little fitted the Africans are to rise in the scale of humanity, and this volume does not belie the conclusion. The tribes around the Zambesi and the Shire, whatever fond enthusiasm may infer, are obviously in a state of barbarism, and show hardly a sign of emerging from it. They roam over one of the gardens of the earth, having never brought it to the uses of man, or even made permanent settlements in it. They are not nations in any sense, with orders, institutions, and government, but mere flocks of aggregated families, under the absolute sway of despotic chieftains. Hardly a trace of any of the arts of life is to be seen in the rude and mean hamlets which form their transitory habitations, and their arms, their dress, and their implements of husbandry, are those of a low class of savage. Their language, with some touches of fancy, is the rude tongue of unreasoning sense; and their religion, with some possible vestiges of traditions of an ennobling kind, is a mass of strange and ignorant superstitions. Though not idolater, as it would appear, their conception of a Supreme Being is essentially that of all barbarians, an omnipotent and vindictive power, and their dull credulity never seems to wander in thought to an invisible world."

The following remarks from Mr. M. Forster, many years an M.P., are full of interest, as the practical experience of fifty years. Mr. Forster informs me that all his efforts to introduce a taste for agricultural industry have signally failed, "from the want of labour and industry in a country where men are superabundant." He also says, "I have had a great many of the native children under my care in England for their education. They learn to read and write, and acquire the other rudiments of education with great quickness and facility, and have considerable receptive, but no creative powers. It is not till they grow up that you discover their natural deficiencies.

"They are capable of attachment, and make excellent servants under strict discipline, but, left to themselves, they are heedless,

yield easily to temptation, and are regardless of future consequences; their thoughts scarcely range beyond the present hour;
at least, these are my impressions, after fifty years' experience
and observation of them. I long indulged sanguine hopes of
native agricultural industry, but time and experience have well-
nigh extinguished them.

" With respect to the religious conversion of the natives, I regret to say that little real progress has been made, notwithstanding the zealous and devoted labours of the missionaries. Within
the limits of the settlements the missionaries have little difficulty
in collecting nominal converts and followers, but the impression
is superficial, and they fail to make their way into the country.
The Christian religion, particularly in its sober Protestant form,
has little to excite the imagination and feelings of a barbarous
people, who fail to appreciate its sublime, religious, and moral
doctrines.

" I may add that I was in Parliament, and a Member of the
Committee that sat on this subject in 1842, and I have seen
little reason to change the opinions I then entertained, except
that my hope in the progress of native industry has since, I am
sorry to say, been rather impaired than strengthened by further
experience and the lapse of time.

" Speaking from my experience, I would say that they are the
worst enemies of the negroes who would give them liberty without being prepared for it. The result of their sudden emancipation in the Southern States will be the extinction of the black
race there, at no distant period.

" Their extinction and sufferings have already begun, and will
proceed at an accelerated pace. The anti-slavery agitators will
soon discover their mistake. Even in the interest of the negro,
they have made a fatal blunder." (January, 1866.)

I will here introduce a few remarks on the republic of Liberia,
a colony, formed on the coast of Africa for liberated slaves, with
the twofold object of modifying the barbarism of the negro aborigines, and giving the freed slave an opportunity of turning his
newly acquired liberty to practical account.

It is a most noteworthy fact that the idea of a colony having
such objects originated with the slaveholders of the United
States, and is a practical reproof to our various religious sects,
which loudly proclaim the doctrine that the virtue, morality,
and benevolence of all the world are centred in themselves.

In 1816 the American Colonization Society was founded. It was of Virginian birth, and was never, therefore, looked upon with favour by the Abolitionists.

The first attempt to colonize was a failure, but in 1822 formal possession was taken of a tract of land thirty-six miles long, by about two miles broad, off Cape Mesurado. For some years the colony steadily increased, under the influence of practical philanthropy, and by the aid of missionaries and schools.

In 1837 there were no less than four societies in America alone, working out the problem of founding a home for liberated slaves and free negroes on the coast of Africa, viz. :—

The American Colonization Society.
The New York Colonization Society.
The Pennsylvania Colonization Society.
The Maryland Colonization Society.

In 1839 the various settlements were consolidated under a new constitution, one part of which was, "that no white man should become a landholder in Liberia," and that "full rights of citizenship should be enjoyed by coloured men alone." This injudicious and narrow-minded step has proved a most serious blow to the prosperity of the settlement.

In 1842, Roberts, an octoroon, was elected governor of the commonwealth of Liberia. In 1847 a declaration of independence was drawn up and proclaimed; and on the 24th August, 1847, the flag of the Republic of Liberia was displayed.

England, France, Prussia, Belgium, and Brazils have acknowledged the independence of this Republic. England presented it with a man-of-war schooner, with armament and stores complete, and English philanthropists vied with Americans in aiding the infant nation, and, among other acts, added to it by purchase the Gallinas territory.

By this acquisition, and that of the Cassa territory in May 1852, Liberia practically extended its dominions from Cape Lahou, eastward of Cape Palmas, to Sierra Leone, about 600 miles.

As regards the full usefulness which might have been expected from the colonization of a portion of Africa by a higher type of the same race, great disappointment has resulted, traceable, for the most part, to the restrictions imposed by the colonists so soon as they were allowed to declare themselves an independent republic; and in a less degree to the inherent repugnance of the negro to till the ground. At this moment, after forty-five years' occupation, the account of land under cultivation is not worth mentioning.

President Roberts was most energetic in rooting out the white element. Thus Liberia cut the ground from under her feet, and I regret to say the prosperity of the Republic has declined from the moment of passing such unwise laws. This is only another proof of the incapability of the negro to run alone, and nothing but the presence of the mixed breeds prevents Liberia from degenerating more rapidly than it does.

The plan of colonizing a part of the coast of Africa by improved negroes is the only solution of the problem—how to utilize the Africans; and if the United States had retained Liberia as a colony, administered by a vigorous white government, it would have proved an untold benefit to the negro race, and most profitable to the United States itself.

Slavery, with the cordial consent of North and South, might have been allowed to die out, while an abundant supply of negro apprentices, under wise and just laws, might have been supplied through Liberian ports; who, after giving, at fair wages, all the aid possible, in a material shape, towards developing their masters' property, and thus, of course, increasing the prosperity of the nation, should, with all the education they were capable of grasping, and, with the fruits of their labour, have been sent back to their native land, to set an example of something better than practising fetish worship, grisgris, murder, rapine, and cannibalism, now flourishing there in the rankest luxuriance.

Perhaps the most startling commentary on this part of my subject, viz. the consideration of the negro on his own soil, will be the news brought by the Royal Mail Steamer 'Athenian,' on the 9th of January from the West Coast of Africa.

"Brass and New Calabar, Nov. 19, 1865.

"Natives of New Calabar made a raid on the Brass men, and returned on the 23rd November with 37 prisoners. On the 24th a great play was held in Calabar Town, and all the prisoners were killed and eaten. The bodies were cut up, and divided among the chiefs according to the numbers taken by each war-canoe."

"Sierra Leone, Dec. 20.

"The native wars in the neighbourhood still continue. At Melliconrie the two great native chiefs Malaghed Bailey and

Bacarry are still fighting with varied success; they have plundered and burnt many factories, the property of British subjects. Atrocities have been committed, vying with those which have recently occurred at Jamaica. All persons captured are at once sold into slavery. No business was done at Sierra Leone."

"At Bathurst a war had broken out at Badahoo, and the natives had threatened the lives of the white population at Bathurst. Messages have been sent from some of the chiefs to the effect that the town would be taken on the 25th December. His Excellency, the Governor, and the merchants, had prepared against any attempt that may be made. Business was at a standstill."

Here then we have the negro in his true colours, committing a series of atrocities, and not, be it remembered, at a small isolated spot on the great African continent, but at various places, extending over 1800 miles. On the 24th November last, we find him murdering his prisoners and devouring their dead bodies at Calabar.

At the same time our pet colony, Sierra Leone,* was witnessing atrocities similar to those perpetrated at Jamaica, while the factories of the English merchants were being burnt and plundered.

Still further north, at Bathurst, the white population were threatened with destruction on the 25th December. A most curious coincidence, to say the least of it, and traceable probably to Jamaica, when the interchange of black troops and frequent communication are taken into account.

I think I have now said sufficient to show that the negro in his own land, and under his own institutions, is little better than a brute,—in mental power a child, in ferocity a tiger, in moral degradation sunk to the lowest depths.

The kings or chiefs, invested with unbounded power, are only exaggerated types of their subjects, and therefore it is fair to infer that social slavery is the effect, not the cause, of this degraded condition.

* Settled in 1787; its chief object the suppression of the slave-trade, religious conversion, and civilization of the natives.

# PART II.

## IN THE NEW WORLD.

AND thus having shown the condition of the negro in the land of his birth, let us now review his status in those parts to which he has been transplanted. In order to this I am here necessarily obliged to touch upon the question of slavery. Slavery, in some form or other, dates from the remotest antiquity; it flourished alike under Pagans, Jews, and Christians. It was an *institution* under the Egyptians, and was especially recognized by the Mosaic law, while, at the beginning of the Christian era, in the city of Rome as many as sixty thousand slaves were living. The serfdom of Russia is a familiar instance in our day.

The ancient custom amongst civilized people of enslaving each other must not be confounded with negro slavery; the "institutions" are widely different. In the one case, men of iron will and determination subjugated their less daring fellow-countrymen, and by their aid made great strides in the civilization of the world, when otherwise progress would have been at a comparative standstill. In the other, a decidedly inferior race was rescued from a state of barbarism scarcely human, and compelled to take a useful position; their right to continue idle spectators of the toil of their fellow-creatures being contrary alike to the laws of God and man.

Certain writers delight to attribute this subjugation to the indulgence of rapacity and force. I differ from this assumption, and take leave to express my belief, that it was rather the result of a rude instinct, well adapted to the conditions of the society in which the institutions respectively flourished.

The most casual observer will not fail to notice, that as education gained ground in any community, so men's minds became enlarged, and they soon found out a means of progression other than enslaving their equals in race. The custom therefore fell into desuetude, until at last it collapsed in the recent abolition of serfdom in Russia, which, looking to the state of advancement in that country compared with the rest of Europe, is as striking an instance of the truth of my remarks as any I could advance.

But, surely, no one can doubt that the institution of slavery has played a very important part in the world's history, or that it has materially aided the progress and advancement of mankind; it is simply falsifying all experience to stigmatize the institution as an unmixed and monstrous evil.

When promiscuous slavery fell into disuse, negro slavery, with which we have now to deal, came into operation. To my mind, this marked a most important epoch in the history of the human race. The practice of making slaves of the negroes arose, doubtless, from two causes; the first being the fact of its prevalence among themselves from time immemorial; the second, that attention was most forcibly drawn to the aptitude of the negro for slavery by the Spanish Wilberforce of three hundred and sixty years ago: I mean, Las Casas.

The Portuguese first procured negroes chiefly from the Guinea coast. As early as 1434 young negroes had been brought to the south of Spain, and sold by one Antonio Gonzales; and thus commenced a traffic, destined in its results to advance civilization at a rate never previously anticipated, and to subdue the American continent in one-tenth the time required by Europe emerge from barbarism.

The importance of this trade being once recognized, the Spaniards eagerly joined in the traffic. They were in fact the prime movers in it.

In 1493 the New World was discovered; and as early as the beginning of the sixteenth century, the destruction of the aboriginal race, wherever the Spaniard planted his foot, began; the disappearance of the races was so rapid, that Las Casas, taking the kindliest interest in the Indian slaves, suggested the employment of negroes in their place. A piece of such singular inconsistency in a philanthropist could hardly be conceived, were not the same peculiarities observable in the imitators of Las Casas at the present day.

c

To give some idea of the rapidity with which the Aborigines disappeared, I may mention, for the benefit of anthropologists, that at the commencement of the sixteenth century, in Hayti alone, the deaths were at the rate of six thousand a year amongst the Indian slaves.

It may be interesting to state that a remarkable decrease of the Aborigines was going on when I was at the Sandwich Islands in 1850, in spite of the number of missionaries established there; and I cannot refrain from recording my experience, in connection with the disappearing of one race before another, that it is not entirely due to the vices of the stronger. A pretty long acquaintance with various savage tribes has convinced me, that though it is quite true that all men are erring, yet, in most cases, it would be difficult to import more vice than is to be found indigenous to the soil.

In 1503 the first negroes crossed the Atlantic; but Herrera, the historian, tells us, that the traffic regularly began in 1510, by order of the King of Spain. It soon became so general that every Spaniard had his negro, who proved of the greatest assistance in consolidating his master's career of conquest.

In 1530 the first insurrection of the blacks occurred in Venezuela, and Herrera says their intention was to murder every white man, while the women were to be apportioned to the rebels. A certain Captain Santiago de Lassada, however, was equal to the emergency, and, with a vigour similar to that of Governor Eyre, stamped out the revolt.

In 1562, the English Government recognized the slave-trade, when the invaluable qualities of the African, in developing new colonies, became apparent; but it was not till 1616 that negroes were imported into Virginia. From that time the traffic became general, and as regards its influence on the future destinies of nations, perhaps, the most important ever undertaken.

About the middle of the eighteenth century, the slave-trade had assumed gigantic proportions. It has been calculated that up to the time of its abolition about twenty millions of negroes had been deported from the African to the American continent,—with how startling a result must be apparent to every thinking mind.

It is impossible to resist the conclusion, which experience and history tend to prove, that, the continuous movement of such a vast body of mankind has been influenced by natural laws, that, the negro has filled the position for which he is fitted by nature, and, that, his services were brought into use when the emergency arose necessitating his employment.

There is something grand, put it as you will, in thus converting the most barbarous and useless population on the earth's surface into active agents for good; the refuse people of the old world aiding in the subjugation of the new,—and all this in less than three hundred years.

At present every habitable part of the New World is divided amongst recognized owners; there is therefore no opening for any enterprising emigrants to snatch from nature large tracts of land; consequently the necessity of perpetuating slavery as constituted at present no longer exists, otherwise the eloquence of any number of negrophilists would have been powerless to destroy the institution.

The Bill introduced into our Parliament for the total abolition of the slave-trade, on and after the 1st January, 1808, received the royal assent on the 25th March, 1807, twenty years after Wilberforce first drew attention to the miseries endured by the negroes on shipboard. But as a still further proof how gradually these movements come about, and that they are rather the effect of natural laws than the result of any particular genius or philanthropy in man, I may mention that the negrophilists of that day do not seem to have considered it a duty to put an end to slavery itself, which, according to common sense, would have been the best process of destroying what they are now pleased to call such a monstrous, unchristian, vile, and indelible stain.

So gradual was the development of feeling on this subject, that the trade was not declared felony until 1811; nor piracy, punishable by death, until 1824; moreover, it is notorious that although the slave-trade even now can hardly be said to have ceased, yet there is on record only a single instance of capital punishment having been inflicted. This proves that the subject was not one of general interest to the public; in fact it has only been kept alive by a certain set of agitators, for the sake of political capital; and very cheaply have they obtained their notoriety, for I know of none of the acknowledged heads of the party who have made themselves practically acquainted with the subject, either on the coast of Africa or the West Indies. If any of them had, like Howard, gone through danger and hardship in the cause, their opinions would have been entitled to respect; but

c 2

as such is not the case, it is to be hoped that the day is approaching when the shallowness of such popularity-mongers will be thoroughly appreciated by the rest of their countrymen.

In 1833 Lord Stanley, then Colonial Secretary, carried a Bill to abolish slavery throughout the British possessions, and thereupon slavery ceased to exist.

Other nations followed our example in putting an end to the slave-trade; but we cannot lay claim to originality in the matter. Ten years before our Bill was passed, when the Spanish-American colonies declared their independence, slavery was abolished, and, in the case of Chili and Peru in particular, in a manner we should have done well to imitate.

At the present moment, Negro slavery is confined to the Spanish and Brazilian possessions. As regards the former, it is announced that the liberation of the slaves will soon take place. It appears that the first tears have been shed in Spain for the negro; while Brazil will doubtless follow the example, although, of all countries, she can least afford to be sentimental, and I do not hesitate to say that the abolition of slavery amongst the present generation of blacks would be full of danger to that empire.

Having thus sketched the course of slavery down to our own time, let us look at the present condition of those who lived under this peculiar institution, after being for nearly a generation in a state of absolute freedom. Although the geographical range of negro slavery has been considerable, I shall show that the negro has not changed his characteristics, whether located under the cold of a northern climate, or the heat of the tropics; and, moreover, that while in slavery he was incomparably better off than he is as a freed man.

Slavery has flourished in Spanish America, the United States, and the West Indies; but of all countries, England has derived the most benefit from it. The slave-trade may emphatically be said to have laid the foundation of our commercial greatness; our cotton aristocracies have been raised upon it; while to it Liverpool and Manchester mainly owe their prosperity.

Never has it fallen to the lot of any savages to enjoy so many opportunities of elevating and improving themselves as the negro. I shall not refer for proof of this to his long connection with ancient civilization, but establish the fact by strictly modern instances.

*Firstly*, we have the case of the free blacks, in the Northern States of America. There they have been settled many years amongst a superior race, greatly exceeding them in numbers, with no other check on their freedom than a feeling that they are in a minority; they are surrounded by educated and industrious people, and have every encouragement to perseverance, both by precept and example.

*Secondly*, we have before us a case of another nature in Hayti. Here the black man, left to his own devices, is absolute as on African soil, without the slightest foreign influence to affect him in any way. Indeed, a white face is as rarely seen in Hayti as a black in London, for the law denying citizenship on any terms to the white man is strictly enforced. In short, the negro does just as he likes, subject to no external control, good or bad.

*Thirdly*, we have to consider his position in the Spanish-American Republics, and in our own possessions in the West Indies, especially in the island of Jamaica. Here in particular his freedom has been secured quite as much as in Hayti; not only that, but he has been incorporated in the body politic on terms of equality with the white man, and as the preponderance of race is in the ratio of nearly forty to one in his favour, no stretch of the imagination can suppose him overshadowed or held in check. In short, the British negro is a citizen in every sense of the word,—on terms of the most perfect equality with the white race, enjoying every privilege which falls to the lot of any other British subject.

In the three cases referred to above, I think we have examples of every phase in which the negro could be placed, so as to test conclusively his power of profiting by the lessons of civilization. But I shall show that he has not been able to engraft himself on a superior civilization, as in the United States; that he has not been able to perpetuate the civilization left to him unconditionally, as at Hayti; and, that he has not been able to acquire a civilization, in spite of the preponderating numbers of his race and a variety of favourable circumstances, as at Jamaica.

Let us first look at some facts in relation to the effect of freedom on the negro. Official returns of the census in the United States are especially valuable in this respect, as showing, from experience, what may be expected in the future, with regard to the millions of slaves lately emancipated; for no one will deny that the negroes freed before the war have had a better chance of engrafting upon themselves some portion of the civilization around them, than their brethren will have, who are just now so suddenly set free.

The census of the United States for 1840, tells us—

1st. That the number of deaf and dumb, blind, idiots, and insane, of the negroes, in the non-slaveholding States, is 1 out of every 96; in the slaveholding States, it is 1 out of every 672; or 7 to 1 in favour of the slaves in this respect, as compared with the free blacks.

2nd. That the number of whites, deaf and dumb, blind, idiots, and insane, in the non-slaveholding States, is 1 in every 561; being nearly 6 to 1 against the free blacks, in the same States.

3rd. That the number of negroes, who are deaf and dumb, blind, idiots, and insane, paupers, and in prison, in the non-slaveholding States, *is* 1 *out of every* 6; and in the slaveholding States, 1 out of every 154; or 22 to 1 against the free blacks, as compared with the slaves.

4th. That taking the two extremes of north and south :—in Maine, the number of negroes returned as deaf and dumb, blind, insane, and idiots, by the census of 1840, *is* 1 *out of every* 12; and in slaveholding Florida, by the same returns, *is* 1 *of every* 1105; or 92 to 1 in favour of the slaves of Florida, as compared with the free blacks of Maine.

This evidence shows the inferiority of the negro, when removed from control, not only to the white man, but even to his fellows in slavery, and should convince negrophilists that their efforts to elevate the negro will ever fail so long as they act upon the unsound theory of equality of races.

The author of 'The Cotton Trade,' Mr. George McHenry, page 258, says :—

"The writer of these pages was born, and has resided nearly all his life, in Pennsylvania, where exists the largest community of free negroes in the world, and he can testify to the gradual decay in their health and morals, as slavery disappeared from the neighbourhood. Neither the laws of the land, nor public societies for his benefit, prevent the African from degenerating.

"Nothing but the controlling influence of a master will keep him from sinking to that barbarous condition which is his natural state. Notwithstanding the attentions and care bestowed upon them by the Quakers, the negroes congregate in certain districts of Philadelphia, live in hovels, and behave in the most disreputable manner."

I must now say a few words with regard to Hayti, where the negro has long enjoyed his freedom. Hayti, or "the land of mountains," was discovered by Columbus in 1492. The island is 390 miles long, by about 100 broad, and contains about nineteen millions of acres, being nearly as large as Ireland. The first European settlement in the New World was commenced on its shores (at Cape Francis) on Christmas Day, 1492.

From an estimated population of one million at that time, the Aborigines were reduced to 60,000 in 1507. In 1508 the first impulse to agriculture was given by the introduction of the sugar-cane by Pedro d'Atenza. In 1511 only 14,000 Indians survived. In 1660 the French obtained a footing on the island, and for thirty years had great difficulty to maintain themselves against the Spaniards, but at the peace of Ryswik Spain ceded the western half to France.

For the next hundred years the French possessions prospered wonderfully, and in 1790 the population amounted to 27,717 whites, 21,800 free men of colour, and 495,528 slaves; total, 555,825 inhabitants under the French flag. On the Spanish side matters had not progressed so favourably, and the population never attained to one-half that of the French.

From the receipt of the news of the French Revolution this prosperity began to decline. A scene of anarchy ensued, such as the world had not seen before. The white republicans of France fought against the white colonists, the black man against his brother, and the mulatto against both.

No wonder that the 50,000 white and coloured men, fighting frantically among themselves, fell an easy prey to the 500,000 slaves. The very *vis inertiæ* of the negroes was sufficient to secure this end, and it is the greatest mistake to attribute their success to heroism, ability, or even soldierly qualities. The fact is, that rapine and murder were the order of the day, just as it is now on the coast of Africa; and by mere force of numbers, the blacks exterminated the whites, so soon as the latter began to quarrel amongst themselves. I will pass over the atrocities of St. Domingo in 1791, with the remark of the historian Alison, that "the cruelties exercised there exceed anything recorded in history. The negroes marched with spiked infants on their spears instead of colours. They sawed asunder their male prisoners, and violated the females on the dead bodies of their husbands." (Vol. ii. p. 240.)

24

From the time (November, 1803) the whites were driven into the sea the island has been the prey to the most frightful anarchy and confusion, folly and brutality, only paralleled, in fact, by its own antecedents, and in the perpetration of which both French and Spanish negroes, on their respective sides of the island, vied with each other in performing such "fantastic tricks"

"Before high heaven, as make tho angels weep."

On the eastern or Spanish side trade and commerce have long ceased to exist; and the ennobling attributes which characterize the negro after sixty years of freedom, has just been exemplified by the sale of his country to the Spanish government, and the revolution which soon after drove the so-called invaders from the country.

With regard to the French negroes, they have tried their hand at Kings, Emperors, and Presidents,—again an Emperor and now another President,—while at one time the French half itself was divided, one section being a kingdom, the other a republic. Revolution has followed revolution in rapid succession. But to bring home to the mind the rapid decadence of the island under the black *régime*, I may instance the state of property in the island under the whites, and its present condition.

In 1789, the French portion of the island contained 793 sugar plantations, 3117 coffee plantations, 789 cotton plantations, and 182 establishments for making rum, besides other minor factories and workshops. At the present time not a tenth part remains, and such cultivation as there is hardly deserves the name; coffee, which requires little or no labour in cultivating, is now almost the sole article of export.

In 1790 the exports were 151,481 tons of produce.

In 1820, the exports had fallen to 16,365 tons!

In short, if it were not for the mulattoes still on the island, all commerce would have long since ceased, and the few remaining plots of reclaimed land become a forest once more. The ruin of Hayti is simply a question of time, as the strict enforcement of the law which declares, "no white man, whatever be his nationality, shall be permitted to land on the Haytian territory with the title of master or proprietor, nor shall he be able in future to acquire there either real estate or the rights of a Haytian," must sooner or later remove every trace of the only element which now keeps its population a degree removed from *barbarism.*

Even between 1860 and 1865 I have noticed the rapid degeneracy; and as soon as the influence of the present civilization expires, so soon will beautiful and fertile Hayti become of no more use to the world than it was before its discovery by Columbus. The aspect of civilization as it now exists there is so ludicrous, that I should often have laughed outright at the antics of the natives, had not the graver feeling of sorrow at seeing such valuable resources so completely thrown away, checked all thoughts of mirth.

To give some idea of the soldiers, I commend to your notice the sketch which I sent from Jacmel last January; it appeared in the 'Illustrated London News,' March 11, 1865.

It will be unnecessary to accumulate proofs of the degradation of the Haytian; late events in connection with the loss of H.M.S. 'Bulldog,' in October last, at Cape Haytien, prove what a pandemonium exists on the island. I shall therefore only quote from a couple of eye-witnesses,—the most impartial, I believe, whom I could select out of numerous authorities, viz. Mr. Walsh, and Lord Eustace Cecil.

Robert M. Walsh, Esq., of Pennsylvania, a commissioner from the United States to Hayti, wrote as follows to Mr. Webster, while Secretary of State :—

" I trust you will pardon me, if I sometimes wander from the serious tone appropriate to a despatch ; but it is difficult to preserve one's gravity with so absurd a caricature of civilization before one's eyes, as is here exhibited in every shape.

" Nothing saves these people from being infinitely ridiculous, but the circumstance of their being often supremely disgusting, by their fearful atrocities. The change from a ludicrous farce to a bloody tragedy, is here as frequent as it is terrible; and the smiles which the former irresistibly provoke, can only be repressed by the sickening sensations occasioned by the latter.

" It is a conviction which has been forced upon me by what I have learned here, that negroes only cease to be children when they degenerate into savages. As long as they happen to be in a genial mood, it is the rattle and the straw by which they are tickled and pleased; and when their passions are once aroused, the most potent weapons of subjugation can alone prevent the most horrible evils.

" A residence here, however brief, must cause the most determined philanthropist to entertain serious doubts of the

possibility of their ever attaining the full stature of intellectual
and civilized manhood, unless some miraculous interposition is
vouchsafed in their behalf.

"In proportion as the recollections and traditions of the old
colonial civilizations are fading away, and the imitative propen-
sity, which is so strong a characteristic of the African, is losing
its opportunities of exercise, the black inhabitants of Hayti are
reverting to the primitive state from which they were elevated
by contact with the whites,—a race whose innate superiority
would seem to be abundantly proved, by the mere fact, that it
is approaching the goal of mental progress, while the other has
scarcely made a step in advance of the position in which it was
originally placed.

"It is among the mulattoes alone, as a general rule, that intelligence and education are to be found; but they are neither
sufficiently numerous, nor virtuous, nor enlightened, to do more
than diminish the rapidity of the nation's descent, and every day
accelerates the inevitable consequence, by lessening their influence and strength.

"In short, the combination of evil and destructive elements
is such, that the ultimate regeneration of the Haytians seems
to me to be the wildest of Utopian dreams. Dismal as this picture may appear, its colouring is not exaggerated. It is as faithful a representation as I can sketch of the general aspect of this
miserable country,—a country where God has done everything to
make his creature happy, and where the creature is doing everything to mar the work of God."

Lord Eustace Cecil, in his article on Hayti, tells us that "the
history of few countries presents such an interminable series of
revolutions, usurpations, and anarchy, as that of Hayti, in the
short period that it has existed as an independent nation."

Speaking of the negroes, he adds:—

"Providence has indeed tempered the wind to the shorn lamb
by giving them few wants, fruitful soil, and a government which
allows those not drawn by the conscription, unrestricted permis-
sion 'to do nothing.' What more could even a discontented
negro wish for? So long as he can lie quietly in the sun, side by
side with his pig on a dungheap, his earthly paradise is attained.

"Take off the general's cocked-hat and epaulets, give him a
hoe, and set him to work in a plantation, and the Maroon negro is
perceptible at once. Tear away the lace and gilding, and you

have the grinning savage. Whet his appetite with a little blood, and Haytian history tells us that he will kill, mutilate, and torture in a fashion that would be worthy of his African ancestors. Dessalines and Christophe excelled even Nero and Domitian in wholesale cruelty."

According to Lord Eustace, the state of finance is verging on bankruptcy. The Haytian greenback, once worth 4*s.* 2*d.*, being now worth only 2¼*d.*, thanks to the black party, headed by the " Emperor Soulouque," " Dukes of Marmalade," and " Counts of Petits Pois."

Lord Eustace concludes his article in the following terms :—

"What more favourable circumstances could the abolitionist wish for to prove his theory of the black man's capacity for self-government ? And what as yet has been the result of the experiment ? Put political considerations entirely aside, and let us merely consider whether the material interests or individual self-improvement of the nation at large, have in the slightest degree progressed. A moment's reflection will convince us to the contrary."

" Slowly and surely will the conviction gain ground, the truth of which has more than once forced itself on men's minds, that moderate subordination to the white man is essential to the happiness of the negro, if he is to become a useful and industrious member of the society in which he lives." (' Impressions of Life at Home and Abroad,' pp. 19 to 75, 1864.)

With regard to the negro population of the Spanish American republics, I am able to speak from a lengthened experience, having spent many years in those countries, in close contact with the people, on the coast as a naval officer, and in the interior as a traveller; and perhaps I shall startle ethnologists when I assert that no true Creole negro any longer exists between Cape Horn and the Mexican empire, although his vices are fully represented by his mixed descendants.

The outward parent characteristics have been more or less obliterated by admixture with the Latin and other races living in those parts of the great American continent at the time freedom was conferred upon the slaves.

In South America,—Chili and Buenos Ayres, for example,—a native negro is unknown. In Bolivia, Peru, and Ecuador the race is largely intermixed with Indian blood (although still bearing the strongly-marked features of the negro), and enjoying an unenviable notoriety as robbers and murderers.

At Lima, Captain Lambert, R.N., was robbed and murdered by these people; Mr. Sulivan, our minister, lost his life; and the late Admiral Sir Henry Bruce, when Commander-in-chief in the Pacific, was stopped in uniform, close to the city, and robbed by a gigantic black native. He was accompanied by his daughter and flag-lieutenant; unfortunately, both himself and the latter were unarmed. However, it may as well be mentioned that their assailant did not long enjoy the impunity offered to crime by the Government of his country, for, making a similar attempt soon after, he was killed on the spot by his intended victim, an Irishman, who happened to have an axe in his hand, unseen by the ruffian.

I mention these incidents, out of numberless cases, to show the reckless depravity which the present race have inherited with their blood, and which is in such marked contrast to the peaceable and orderly conduct of the Indian population surrounding them.

In Central America, at New Granada, the Mosquito coast, and British Honduras, the negroes approach much nearer to the pure type than can be found in South America, as their numbers are being constantly recruited from the West Indian Islands, either for mahogany-cutting or transit purposes. With regard to the negro of Panama, I can only say that a more turbulent, vicious, insolent, and lazy miscreant does not exist on the face of the earth.

In Costa Rica and Nicaragua I have seen but one native negro, and only a few instances of people with perceptible African blood in their veins. The same is the case in San Salvador, Guatemala, and Honduras, except on the Atlantic coast of the two latter Republics, where, owing to the migrations from the West India islands, alluded to before, the stock has been more or less preserved.

The Spanish-American colonists have held the negro in slavery from the time of Columbus to within the last forty years, and therefore a lengthened experience of his character will not be denied to them. Their feeling on this matter will be best understood by the facts of their unanimous rejection of the late President Lincoln's attempt to introduce freed negroes as settlers on their territory; and subsequently (and I mention this to show how deliberate and confirmed is the feeling) by the *attempt to* insert in a concession for a transit across Central

America, between the Atlantic and Pacific, which I have just obtained from Congress, a clause to the following effect, viz. that no negro could become a citizen of the Republic, nor hold real estate on any pretence whatever. Such a clause, however sensible in some respects, would have had an injurious effect upon *my* enterprise in more ways than one, and therefore, after considerable discussion, it was erased; but the incident serves to show the sentiments of a republican Congress, with regard to the worth of the negro as a citizen, and is valuable as proving the unanimity of practical men, of whatever nationality, on this subject.

We have now to consider the condition of the negro in the West Indies. These islands offer a wide range for comparison, and ample means for proving that the negro, in his small way, is more civilized, and altogether better, where a controlling influence is exercised—at Barbadoes for example; yet I shall take it for granted that this is well understood by all who do not wilfully shut their eyes to the truth.

It will be sufficient therefore, for my present purpose, to describe that negro elysium, the island of Jamaica, in order to show that the negro is a negro still, theories to the contrary notwithstanding.

Jamaica, or the "Land of Streams," is nearly 150 miles in length, by an average of 40 in breadth, and contains 2,750,000 acres of land. The country is beautifully picturesque, and the view from some of the hills compares favourably, in my opinion, with the lovely Vega of Granada, as seen from the Alhambra. The eastern end of the island is mountainous, and in many places thickly covered with forest. The western is more level, and here the only railroad has been built (1845),—the Kingston and Spanish Town.

Jamaica was settled by the Spaniards in 1510, and remained in their possession about one hundred and fifty years. On its capture, 3rd May, 1655, by Admiral Penn and General Venables, there were only 1500 Spaniards and Portuguese and the same number of negroes and mulattoes on the island; not a trace of the Aborigines could be found. I commend this fact to the negrophilists, who declaim about the atrocities of the *"Aboriginal Maroons,"* little thinking that they are talking of a race identical with that which they have petted into insurrection.

The Maroons, whose name is a corruption of the Spanish

Cimarones—wild men, are simply runaway slaves from Cuba and Jamaica itself: negroes, in point of fact, neither more nor less; settled on land assigned to them in 1738.

The case of these Maroons is another instance of how little the possession of mere freedom can affect the civilization of a savage people. They have been free since the English took possession of the island, and what is now their condition? Have they in any one sense become useful members of the community? Every one knows they have not. They roam, half naked, in the woods, and make their women do every sort of drudgery.

The Constitution of Jamaica is modelled upon that of the mother-country. The Queen is represented by the Governor; the House of Lords, by a Council of Twelve appointed by the Sovereign; the House of Commons, by an Assembly, consisting of forty-five members—two for each of the twenty-one parishes, and one for each of the three towns, Spanish Town, Kingston, and Port Royal.

The franchise is based on a £6 freehold, and is therefore open to every one. All appointments are made without reference to colour. The whites and blacks are governed by the same laws.

So much has been written about the Jamaica negro, both for and against him, up to the period of emancipation in 1833, and the sudden termination of the apprenticeship system in 1838, that it will be needless to give any detailed description prior to that period.

I will merely remark, that in early days the prosperity of Jamaica, in a purely commercial sense, was considerable; and to give an idea of the capacity of the island for agriculture alone, I may mention that, besides a large annual amount of other produce, in 1797, 7,869,138 lbs. of ginger was exported; in 1805, 150,352 hogsheads of sugar; in 1814, 34,045,585 lbs. of coffee; in 1832, 19,815,010 lbs. pimento.

At the present time sugar has fallen off to 30,000 hogsheads; coffee, to 8,000,000 lbs.; pimento the same; while of ginger only 650,000 lbs. have been raised.

For the last thirty years the attention of the general public has been but little attracted to Jamaica affairs; the insurrection in 1832 brought the island into as much notice at that time, as the present one has now; but during the intervening thirty-four years the negrophilists have had it all to themselves, and every opportunity has been afforded them of proving practically the soundness or otherwise of the views, they have so loudly proclaimed, viz. that the absolute liberty, and the enjoyment of all the rights and privileges of British subjects, by the negro, would prove his equality with the white man, beyond question or cavil.

Nowhere could a better field have offered itself to try the experiment, than in Jamaica, the most important possession of the British Crown in the West Indies, with ample territory, a fertile soil, and a large population. Let us examine the result.

And first I would say a few words in reference to my personal experience at Jamaica.

The most striking peculiarity is the abandoned profligacy of the coloured races. Port Royal and Kingston, in this respect, are sinks of iniquity. Religion struck me as being at a very low ebb everywhere. I remember in 1860 that the bishop was compelled to reject the entire class assembled for confirmation at Manchioneal. The native Baptist revivals and prayer-meetings, if they had not excited in me a feeling of deep sorrow at the depravity and hypocrisy which marked the proceedings, would have been simply ludicrous, the screaming and chattering being more characteristic of a meeting of monkeys than like an assemblage of men and women, and I am not surprised at the evident anxiety of the leading Baptists in this country to disclaim any spiritual connection with their black pupils in Jamaica. In short, the unchecked depravity of the negro crops out on every side, details of which would be quite unfit for publication, and which must be seen to be believed.

Of the sloth of the negro there is unfortunately but too abundant evidence, in the desolation of whole districts containing the richest lands, and in abandoned estates with their costly works in ruins, and not a sign of human industry as far as the eye can reach; but if that is not considered proof sufficient, the condition of the poor women will illustrate better than anything else the injurious effect of unlimited freedom on men utterly unfit to appreciate its value. All the hard labour in the fields falls upon the women, and a sketch sent by me to the ' Illustrated London News,' November 25, 1865, page 512, ' Coaling a Royal Mail Steam Packet at Kingston, Jamaica,' will show that the custom is not confined to the plantations, but extends to the hardest kind of labour in the towns, and points out more clearly than any words of mine the degraded position of the negress and the disgraceful sloth of her lord and master. I commend this sketch to the notice of the would-be friends of the black race at Jamaica.

Dr. Underhill has put himself forward as an authority on this subject, and has thought proper to suggest what ought to be done, it will therefore be the best plan to examine how far his opinions are correct.

In 1859–60, Dr. Underhill and the Rev. Mr. Brown visited Jamaica as a deputation from the Baptist Missionary Society. Their tour was a wonderful instance of Anglo-Saxon energy and perseverance, taking the heat of the climate into consideration. During four months they travelled all over the island, holding about eighty meetings.

Now as the negroes were fully informed of Dr. Underhill's expected appearance, they attended each meeting in great numbers, dressed in their best, and many of the men well-mounted. Those who arranged this programme could as safely count upon a great concourse of excitable negroes, who would naturally flock to see the Baptist minister from England, as their brethren in England could count upon filling Exeter Hall by the sensational placard announcing eight miles of dead bodies in Jamaica. In fact, during Dr. Underhill's stay, it was quite a series of sight-seeing for the negroes; and that all things appeared *couleur de rose* to him, is proved by the following estimate of their wealth in his ' West Indies,' p. 421 :—

|  | £. | s. | d. |
|---|---|---|---|
| 65,000 houses of furniture at £16 . . | 1,040,000 | 0 | 0 |
| 354,575 acres of land at 30s. . . . . | 531,862 | 10 | 0 |
| Clothes for 65,000 families at £4 each . | 260,000 | 0 | 0 |
| Stock on freeholds at £3 each family . | 195,000 | 0 | 0 |
| 5000 sugar-mills at £10 each . . . . | 50,000 | 0 | 0 |
| Funds in savings-banks . . . . . . | 49,399 | 0 | 0 |
| Grand total . | £2,126,261 | 10 | 0 |

Such an estimate could no doubt be made by the most conscientious man, after seeing crowds of well-mounted negroes and well-dressed negresses, collected every day to hear and see him, and boasting, as is their wont, of the amount each one possessed in lands and money; but the estimate is as deceptive as the appearances upon which it is based.

I have never seen a negro hut worth £16, in any part of the island. Generally it is of the very rudest description. Again, land at 30*s*. per acre! why, half that amount would be considered by many a proprietor a perfect godsend for the purchase of his estate.*

The clothes, no doubt, average £4 per family; for finery in dress is a passion with the negro, and both men and women make it their first consideration to appear on high-days and holidays in gorgeous apparel.

Stock I should divide by half, and then it would be above the average. As to the sugar-mills, they are of the rudest description, mere presses, and would not yield an average of £2 each.

The amount in the savings-banks, I doubt; for negroes, as a rule, do not adopt the system; but supposing Dr. Underhill's estimate to be correct, how can the theory of the late deep distress and crime arising from poverty, with such a large fund to draw upon, be sustained? The truth is, that such amounts as were deposited increased rather than diminished, during the drought. How then can he say, "All accounts, both public and private, concur in affirming the alarming increase of crime, chiefly of larceny and petty theft. *This arises from the extreme poverty of the people*"?

Besides, it must be remembered, that while Dr. Underhill met with nothing but flattery from the negroes, and while the

---

* "5, *Lime Street Square, London, E.C., Dec. 26th*, 1865.

"Sir,—It has occurred to me that as none of the wealthy members of the Anti-Slavery Society (Mr. Alexander, Mr. Buxton, Mr. Gurney, and others) own an acre of land in Jamaica, or have one shilling depending on the prosperity of the island, they might like to take a more practical interest in its welfare, and make an investment in the soil by purchasing the estate of which I send you a plan. It consists, you will observe, of more than 1000 acres of land, which are situated close to the sea; it is well watered, has sugar-works, and a very fair house on it. For this property, together with nearly 100 head of stock on it, I am willing to take £2500. There are a great many small negro freeholders residing in the immediate neighbourhood, and altogether I should think it would be an admirable locality for the practical development of the Anti-Slavery Society's philanthropic views. I may add that the title I can give is unexceptionable, it having been bought some time ago under the provisions of the Encumbered Estates Act. May I ask you to return me the plan should none of the gentlemen connected with the Society be inclined to entertain my proposition? "I am, etc.,

"(Signed) W. B. WATSON.

"*L. A. Chamerovzow, Esq.*"

dark side of their character was carefully kept from view, he probably had no opportunity of hearing the other side of the question, by mixing with the higher classes. It so happens, that I was at Jamaica while Dr. Underhill was there, and I am sorry to say that many excellent friends of mine, most liberal-minded men in other respects, were prejudiced enough to inform me, that they cordially agreed with Mr. Anthony Trollope in "hating Baptists like poison," and would as soon think of admitting them to social intercourse as of allowing their black servants to sit at table with them; because they constantly opened the old sore, and revived the antagonism of the races on every occasion. The opinion has been expressed to me a hundred times, that, what with the Assembly and the Baptists,* the island was doomed.

The deduction I draw from what has now been said is, that the negro in a state of freedom continues powerless to advance himself in civilization, and that he is most improvable when under moderate control. It is no longer expedient to make a slave of him; he has performed his part in the world's history in that capacity; and even as he superseded a weaker system of labour, the slavery of the ancients, so Watt and Stephenson have surely and for ever emancipated him by the introduction of an agency more powerful still.

He has no right, however, and civilized man has no right to allow him, to pass his existence without in any way contributing to the advancement of mankind.

I believe that a system of hiring labour for five years from the coast of Africa, would not only be advantageous to the employers, but would be a boon to the labourer himself, and would, in due course, humanize his fellow-countrymen at home; it

---

* This dislike and distrust of the Baptists is not sectarian, because other religious sects are loved and admired by the whites. "The Moravians sent out a mission to the West Indies in 1732, and in 1787 they had ministers in Antigua, St. Kitts, Barbadoes, and Jamaica, as well as in Surinam and the Danish Islands. These humble and zealous men, with the very limited means at their command, have been deservedly successful; the simplicity of their manners, and the equal simplicity of the tenets they inculcated, being eminently fitted to impress the hearts of an uncivilized people with feelings of kindness and brotherly love, without exciting those *frightful horrors*, the primary object of their Baptist successors, and which, grafted on African superstition, cannot fail, sooner or later, to produce lamentable results." ('Slavery in the West Indies.')

should be made compulsory, perhaps, at the expiration of the term, to return the negro to the place he had left. In every other respect the business should be conducted on the broadest principles of free-trade. This plan is nothing new; it answers well with the Krumen on the coast, and the Seedeys of India; indeed, at present, the available supply exceeds the demand.

I make bold to say that 50,000,000 of blacks have not been placed on this magnificent globe of ours for no purpose; it is therefore our duty, by wise legislation, to utilize this large mass of human beings. They must be dealt with from no sentimental standpoint, but from a knowledge of their nature and characteristics, discarding at once the theory of equality. We do not admit equality even amongst our own race, as is proved by the state of the franchise at this hour in England ! and to suppose that two alien races can compose a political unity is simply ridiculous. One section *must* govern the other.

I cannot see any hardship to the negro in deferring the claims of the negrophilists for equality on the part of their idol, until he has done what every man amongst us is obliged to do, viz. *prove his title* before he is admitted into fellowship.

In concluding, I would remark, that what I have said on this vexed question is the practical conviction of twenty-five years' experience of the negro in all parts of the world. I have commanded negroes in Her Majesty's Service. I have had negroes in my private employment, in a country where I had but to lift my finger to have them punished as I liked; and I have controlled them where the law was in their own hands. From negroes I have exacted hard labour, such as would be thought considerable anywhere; but *not* at the expense of affecting equality with them. It has been entirely by an opposite course that I have succeeded in making eminently useful and warmly attached to me, many individuals of a race which, I believe, by a like course, and it only, can be trained to obedience and industry, and thus become useful members of society.

---

At this point Captain Pim paused, and observed that the remaining portion of his paper referred exclusively to the recent insurrection of negroes in Jamaica, and he asked the President to take the sense of the meeting whether he should proceed with it or not.

The PRESIDENT observed that the paper had been referred—as was customary with papers read before their Society—to referees, to determine whether it was suitable to be read, and they had reported that portions of it were not strictly anthropological. The Council had carefully considered the subject, but were divided in opinion, and under those circumstances it had been decided to leave it to the meeting to determine whether they wished to hear the remarks of Captain Pim on the subject of the insurrection in Jamaica. He would therefore take a show of hands on the question. (On a show of hands, it was found that, with the exception of *one* person, the meeting was unanimous that the rest of the paper should be read.)

# PART III.

## JAMAICA.

I now come to the consideration of some of the facts in connection with the late insurrection at Jamaica. The story is so familiar that it is not necessary to go much into details. I shall merely, therefore, touch upon those points which seem to me to require some explanation, and which have been so much misunderstood by those who, when urging upon the Government the suspension of Governor Eyre, added their pious hope that it would be " by the neck."

And first, with respect to Governor Eyre's despatch; for that document contains the clue to all the subsequent outcry. His Excellency does not hesitate to attribute the blame to Dr. Underhill and the Baptists. Whether he is right or not, one thing is certain, that this charge has caused the present excitement on the subject; for it is clear that the colonists themselves, who ought to be the best judges, admire the energy and vigour with which Governor Eyre acted, and approve the measures he took, as the following recent testimony from Jamaica will show :—

The 'Colonial Standard' says :—"The intelligence by this mail is well calculated to excite the surprise and sorrow, and to arouse the deepest apprehensions of the colonists. Yielding to the ferocious clamours of the anti-slavery party in England, her Majesty's ministers have thought fit to supersede Mr. Eyre, and to place him before the Jamaica rebels in the humiliating position of a suspected criminal awaiting trial. It is useless to disguise the fact, that this proceeding will have a very dangerous effect on the minds of the disaffected people of this island. Already the people have imbibed the notion that the Governor is to be tried and hanged for murder, especially the murder of George

William Gordon; and those who know the negro character will understand that it will be impossible hereafter to make them believe the contrary. Mr. Eyre is virtually in disgrace by the very nature of the position in which he is placed, and so far, at all events, he is punished already through a prejudgment of his case by parties who start off, in their demands for justice against him, by asserting that he punished the rebels without a fair trial.

"Every one knows that we have been determined opponents of Mr. Eyre's administration, and that we have over and over urged his recall on the British Government. We opposed him, however, on correct principles. He did not, in our opinion, by his acts exhibit the peculiar qualities necessary in the ruler of a free country. Under any other circumstances we could rejoice at his removal, as a triumph to the opinions we have always conscientiously advocated; but common gratitude for the sincere and efficient manner in which he put down the rebellion, and sympathy against the injustice which is done to him in return, no less than a deep apprehension of the probable effect of the proceeding on the minds of beings, so well known to us as the negroes, force us to denounce the treatment he has received as unwarranted by justice or prudence.

"The appointment of Sir Henry, as it will be seen, virtually supersedes our present highly popular and beloved commander of the forces, Major-General O'Connor, C.B., *ad interim* it may be; but such a circumstance will, we are certain, find no favour in the country among any class of persons. It is felt by all that Major-General O'Connor, instead of the slight which he experiences from her Majesty's Government in deference to the enemies of this island, ought to have, on the contrary, received the highest approbation of the sovereign, to which his late services in this island have pre-eminently entitled him.

"Exeter Hall having carried the day, it is hardly of any use to waste words in disputing against the vile calumnies which the votaries of the faith preached there have heaped upon the upper classes and the authorities of this country. Every man of judgment will take assertions coming from such a quarter for what they are worth. We must make allowance for human infirmities, and we cannot expect that whilst even sincere philanthropists are never able to see more than one side of any subject, the negro-maniacs of Exeter Hall would be free from the same fault. Müller found people to doubt his guilt, and no commission, no proof, will ever convince the maniacs in question that the negro can be wrong, or the white man right. But the British people are about to be brought face to face with the negro through the investigations about to take place, and a spirit of inquiry has been aroused in England and elsewhere, which will surely lead to such knowledge as will enable a true estimate of the negro character to be formed. Both the planter and the negro may then hope for justice from a better-informed public opinion in reference to them than previously existed. We shall simply confine ourselves to noticing certain matters that have come out since the sailing of the last packet."

I have now to make a few remarks on Dr. Underhill's notorious letter. But I shall only refer to the part where these words occur: "I shall say nothing of the course taken by the Jamaica Legislature," (and then consistently enough) "of their *abortive* immigration bills, of their *unjust* taxation of the *coloured population*, of their refusal of *just* tribunals, of their *denial of political rights* to the *emancipated negroes.*"

Such words are harmless enough when uttered in this country; but their effect is very different upon excitable negroes, strong in a preponderance of forty to one over the whites.

It has been said, why publish such a firebrand? This question is easily answered. It was the safest course, taking measures at the same time for the public safety. Had no notice been taken of the letter, the Baptist missionaries would doubtless have published it themselves, and possibly in an aggravated form. We have a case in point in the manifesto sent to the Maories the other day by the "Aborigines Protection Society," which New Zealand colonists, who certainly ought to understand the natives, declare has been the means of prolonging the war, with a cost of many valuable lives to both sides.

The next point to which I would draw attention is the fact that the insurrection which took place at Morant Bay, on the 11th, had been brewing in that vicinity since the 7th, and was not therefore the outburst of a sudden indignant appeal for justice. The proofs are abundant; and when to this is added, as the Governor tells us, that he had been compelled some months prior to the outbreak to send vessels of war to various parts of the island to overawe disaffection, it is quite clear that the occurrences we so much deplore at Morant Bay can be designated by no other name than rebellion. Nobody on the island doubted, and no one at home on calm reflection can doubt, that the Governor had to deal with a rebellion as serious as its three predecessors, and not a mere riot. Paul Bogle regularly marshalled his forces, administering a fearful oath to his followers and to the police, sent to make certain arrests, but whom he made prisoners as early as the 9th October. On the 11th, *before* proceeding to the Court House, the police station was sacked, and the arms secured; and finally, the rebels *commenced* the attack themselves, the volunteers with wonderful forbearance desisting from firing until it became a question of life and death. There can, therefore, be no doubt that the outbreak was the premature commencement of a rebellion, and that the slightest hesitation on the part of the Governor would have been a fatal mistake.

The proclamation of martial law became an absolute necessity : no sane man would have dreamt of hesitating : and it was not proclaimed a minute too soon. The clamour, therefore, which has arisen can only result from ignorance of martial law and the inevitable results, viz. the horrors of war intensified by civil commotion, which the insurgents clearly brought on themselves; I have had some little experience in these matters, and I will endeavour to explain in what manner martial law and courts martial are understood by naval and military men.

I observe that my countrymen generally confound martial law with courts martial; but there cannot be a greater mistake. The latter is the law applied to the trial of naval and military men who voluntarily make themselves amenable to it, by the act of joining the respective services. It is written law based on the Articles of War and the Mutiny Acts, and also on " the custom of the service," to use the technical term.

Martial law, on the contrary, is, in fact, the absence of law. The Duke of Wellington's definition is clear, and like everything that has emanated from that great man, to the purpose.

" Martial law," he says, " is neither more nor less than the will of the general who commands the army : in fact, martial law means no law at all; therefore the general who declares martial law, and commands that it should be carried into execution, is bound to lay down the rules, regulations, and limits, according to which his will is to be carried out."

There is no doubt that Government has the power of proclaiming martial law, to meet an attack against law and order.

Much stress has been laid on the *lengthened* continuance of martial law at Jamaica, but it must be borne in mind that the whites were out-numbered forty to one, and that a long time was required to *ensure* the safety of the country, because the mountains, forests, and impassable rivers afforded shelter to the rebels, who could, while the slightest organization remained, at any time renew their attempt at rebellion, as in 1760.

As a case in point, and one which has been strangely overlooked, the following proclamation of Paul Bogle's was found, dated the day *after* the Governor considered the insurrection at an end. For that is the interpretation put upon his despatch; but His Excellency evidently meant, crushed out in the districts *under his eye;* and he no doubt felt the keenest anxiety to prevent its making head in the woods by the severe and necessary measures he adopted.

Subjoined is a copy of the document found by Lieut. Oxley :—

"Morant Bay, Oct. 17.

"Mr. Graham and other Gentlemen,—It is time for us to help ourselves skin for skin. The iron bar is now broken in this parish. The white people send a proclamation to the Governor to make war against us, which we all must put our shoulder to the wheels and pull together. The Maroons sent the proclamation to meet them at Hayfield at once without delay—that they will put us in the way how to act. Every one of you must leave your house—take your guns; who don't have guns, take cutlasses. Down at once! Come over to Stony Gut, that we might march over to meet the Maroons at once without delay. Blow your shells! roule your drums! house to house; take out every man; march them down to Stony Gut; any that you find, take them in the way; take them down with their arms; war is at my black skin; war is at hand from to-day till to-morrow. Every black man must turn out at once, for the oppression is too great. The white people are now cleaning up their guns for us, which we must prepare to meet them too. Cheer, men! Cheer in heart; we looking for you a part of the night or before daybreak.—We are, yours truly,

"(Signed)   PAUL BOGLE,    J. G. M'LAREN,
              B. CLARKE,     P. CAMERON.

"Get a bearer to send us an answer to this, for they determine to make us slaves again. When you do come to Stony Gut or Hayfield, blow your shells, and tell what place you in from before entered. . "E. K. BAILEY."

I may mention another fact not generally known, that a few hours' delay in appealing to the Maroons, and inducing them to join the white men, would have resulted in their going over in a body to the rebels, who were only too anxious to obtain their co-operation, as this proclamation shows. Moreover, to show how insecure was the peace of the island when the Governor wrote his despatch, and, therefore, how necessary it was to continue martial law, a plot was discovered on the 17th, to seize the town (Morant). The instigator, E. K. Bailey, a black man, one of Her Majesty's volunteers, a sergeant of St. Thomas's-in-the-East Company, wrote to Paul Bogle on the 17th, telling him that only a few blue-jackets were left, and that it could be easily taken.

A strong force started for Morant Bay on the 18th, at two A.M., for Stony Gut, to attack the place; but Bogle and his men had left, and the place was entirely abandoned. Bogle's proclamation, however, was found, dated the day before (17th) by Lieut. C. L. Oxley, H.M.S. Wolverine.

Another point on which I shall no doubt be expected to say a few words, is the trial and execution of G. W. Gordon.

Governor Eyre was compelled to arrest this man, not merely from the conviction forced on his own mind that he was deeply implicated as the prime mover of the revolt, but from the unanimous opinion of his guilt; and when his Excellency returned to Kingston from Morant Bay, his surprise was great that G. W. Gordon had not already been arrested; but as soon as he saw, by the admission of those around him, General O'Connor, Dr. Bowerbank, and others, that it had been put off from fear of an outbreak at Kingston, the Governor gave another proof of his courage and determination, by ordering the arrest to be made at once.

That the Kingston authorities had good ground for their apprehensions, is proved by the fact that the troopers had to draw pistols while surrounding the carriage containing the prisoner, driven as fast as possible, so as not to allow a population—insolent and lawless as any in the world—time to organize a rescue.

The removal of Mr. Gordon from Kingston to St. Thomas's-in-the-East, was in strict accordance with the laws of the land; and, moreover, General O'Connor expressly says that he had not a soldier to preserve the peace, and which could not have been maintained had the trial taken place at Kingston; and it is hard to see what other step the Governor could have taken under the circumstance. The unanimity of all classes, black and white, in pointing to Mr. Gordon as the real instigator of the rebellion, is, to say the least of it, most telling against him.

And now with respect to the court-martial by which he was tried. I may mention that of the two courts sitting for the trial of prisoners, one composed of three militia officers, the other of two naval officers and an ensign in the army, the latter was selected; first, because it was composed of officers of higher rank; and secondly, because the impartiality of its members could be relied on; officers of the island militia, of course knowing Mr. Gordon well, and holding strong opinions against him.

Various remarks have been made about midshipmen and boys trying prisoners. I will just remark, *en passant*, that a commander in the navy ranks with a lieutenant-colonel in the army; a lieutenant, eight years, with a major; a junior lieutenant, with a captain in the army; so that the trial took place before officers of sufficiently high rank; and as regards their youth, I may state that the average age was twenty-eight.

I am sure that the officers of the court were most solemnly impressed with their responsibility; and that had there been a shadow of a doubt as to his guilt, Gordon would not have been executed; he was listened to patiently in defence for *two hours*, and courts martial, as I can personally testify, are not usually famous for spinning out trials.

In respect to Mr. Gordon himself, I will say very few words. There is, of course, a strong and proper feeling amongst gentlemen against unveiling the errors and delinquencies of a man who has gone to account before another Tribunal, but I may remark that the letter of Mr. Gordon to Mr. Chamerovzow, which that gentleman read at Exeter Hall, roundly abusing Mr. Eyre in sufficiently coarse terms, and asserting that he obtained a piano with his ill-gotten wealth, and the following extracts from his speeches in the Assembly, will give some idea of the lengths to which this Baptist demagogue could go in exciting his ignorant hearers, and the falsehoods he was capable of uttering.

A few passages will suffice. *" Per se,"* as the hon. member for St. Catherine said, "the people would be quite right to break out into open rebellion. If an illegality is permitted in the Governor, an illegality may be permitted on the part of the people. . . . I have never seen an animal more voracious for cruelty and power than the present Governor of Jamaica. . . . If we are to be governed by such a Governor much longer, the people will have to fly to arms and become self-governing."

At the trial, Mr. Gordon, in cross-questioning a witness, uses these words, "Are you aware that I have been corresponding with Paul Bogle for years?" and again, in his defence, distinctly states, that "Paul Bogle is certainly my political friend." Yet in his letter to his wife, written, it is said, one hour before his execution, he distinctly asserts, " I knew nothing of the man Bogle." There are only two ways of accounting for this inconsistency : either a pious fraud has been perpetrated in the publication of that letter, or instead of being a type of the martyr St. Stephen, Mr. Gordon ought, perhaps, to be classed with men like Müller. There are, however, instances in history where letters of a similar character *have* been written just before execution. He had thirty-six hours at least for preparation, and was not therefore hurried to execution, as will be seen by reference to the date of sentence, delivered in the presence of the prisoner, on Saturday, October 21, the evening of the day of trial :—

"The Court, having heard the prisoner's defence, also the witness he called in his defence, consider the charges proved most fully, and do therefore adjudge the prisoner, George William Gordon, to be hung by the neck until he be dead, at what time and place the Brigadier-General may direct.

"H. Brand, President, Lieutenant, Royal Navy.

"Morant Bay, Oct. 21, 1865."

"Approved and confirmed.

"Moreover, I fully concur in the sentence awarded, such being fully borne out by the evidence.

"The prisoner to be hung on Monday next, the 23rd of October, 1865 ; to-morrow, the 22nd, being Sunday, *and the state of this part of the country* not rendering it necessary to inflict the punishment on the Sabbath-day.

"A. A. Nelson, Brigadier-General,

"Commanding Field Forces.

"Morant Bay, Oct. 21, 1865, 8 p.m."

Great stress has been laid on the conduct of the officers engaged in quelling the rebellion : this arises from the inability of
people at home to understand the excitement of men engaged in
peculiarly hazardous and trying service. Groping about the bush
after armed rebels, requires more nerve than to go through a
pitched battle; but people at home cannot realize this, and because no lives were lost, think the service child's play. A mere
handful of whites amongst thousands of disaffected blacks, is not
child's play.

I will take the case of Colonel Hobbs, for example.

Colonel Hobbs, of the 6th Royals, an enthusiastic soldier, and
a man of sterling piety, a living example of an officer and a
Christian, has been pronounced "a ruffian;" the privates of his
regiment, and the experience of his officers, alike testify that he
is incapable of an unkind or hasty word, or ungenerous action ;
and that such summary justice as he inflicted, resulted from the
desperate nature of the situation. The case of " Paul Bogle's
valet" has been extensively used against this much-maligned
officer, under the impression that the valet was a mere lad of
tender age, who denounced everybody, in mortal terror of his own
life : the truth is, he was a married man with two children.
The term 'boy' is a common expression in the West Indies for
even old men.

So far from carrying out his duty in a bloodthirsty spirit,
Colonel Hobbs actually prayed with the culprits himself when
the services of a minister of religion could not be procured.

I have now only to say a few words in relation to the part the
Government at home has taken in this matter.

Governor Eyre will be the greatest sufferer; on his devoted
head will descend all the wrath of Exeter Hall and its followers;
and although he will doubtless come out of the furnace un-
scathed in reputation, yet the anxiety and trouble he is now enduring must make him an old man before his time. Little did
he think, when the news of Lord Palmerston's death reached
Jamaica, that he, of all men, would soon have bitter cause to
regret the loss of a statesman who never turned his back on a
loyal and dutiful public servant.

To the thinking Englishman and true lover of his country, a
lesson has been taught of no small import,—by a withdrawal of
the curtain which usually shuts out from public view the weak-
nesses, follies, and vacillations of official routine.

In the conduct of Jamaica affairs we have laid ourselves open to the sneers of both Europeans and Americans, and no one can foresee what mischief may accrue to us from the exhibition lately witnessed in high quarters.

In reply to Governor Eyre's report, a despatch is sent approving his conduct, but before that approval reaches its destination, orders are forwarded to suspend him. Deputations wait on Ministers, and scenes of "rowdyism," to say the least of it, are permitted, such as would not be tolerated in the weakest republic.

If walls have ears, how they must have tingled at the brow-·beating and coarse wit inflicted on a Cabinet Minister, especially if the said walls could remember the scene in the same place, so graphically described in the 'Morning Star' in the following words :—" In the early part of 1830, as we have heard the story, a deputation of Reformers waited upon the Duke of Wellington. They came to represent to him the imperative necessity of some move on the part of the Ministry to satisfy the public demand. Unless this be done, ' we cannot,' said the spokesman, 'answer for the preservation of peace.' 'And pray, Sir,' said the grim old soldier, 'who asked you to answer for it ? We,' he added, with a grimly significant smile, ' can answer for it ourselves.' The astonished deputation were for abandoning the conference thus sharply interrupted. As they were moving to the door, silent and angered, the Duke recalled them. ' Gentlemen,' he said—and perhaps they expected some conciliatory observation— ' you have your heads on your shoulders now—have the wisdom to keep them there.' "

The day is, perhaps, gone by for a similar display of vigour on the part of Ministers; but surely the people of this mighty nation, foremost in the world, have a right to expect dignity and self-respect in their chiefs, and consistency in their Government, even if that Government has not the ability to understand how hazardous it is to vacillate with savages, and what a death-blow it is to that confidence in Governmental support which should animate naval, military, and civil chiefs, serving their country in responsible positions abroad.

There have been no less than *four* serious and *ten* minor insurrections in Jamaica in about a hundred years; one in 1760, another in 1795, the third in 1832, and the most memorable in October last. To show that they all have a similar complexion, I subjoin the following account of a negro rising in Jamaica 105 years ago, and which will be read with interest at the present juncture. It is extracted from Smollett's history :—

"While the British commanders exerted themselves by sea and land with the most laudable spirit of vigilance and courage against the foreign adversaries of their country, the colonists of Jamaica ran the most imminent hazard of being extirpated by a domestic enemy. The negro slaves of that island, grown insolent in the contemplation of their own formidable numbers, or by observing the supine indolence of their masters, or stimulated by that appetite for liberty so natural to the mind of man, began, in the course of the year, to entertain thoughts of shaking off the yoke by means of a general insurrection. Assemblies were held, and plans resolved for this purpose. At length they concerted a scheme for rising in arms all at once in different parts of the island, in order to massacre all the white men, and take possession of the Government. They agreed that this design should be put into execution immediately after the departure of the fleet for Europe, but their plan was defeated by their ignorance and impatience. Those of the conspirators that belonged to Captain Forest's estate, being impelled by the fumes of intoxication, fell suddenly upon the overseer while he sat at supper with some friends, and butchered the whole company. Being immediately joined by some of their confederates, they attacked the neighbouring plantations, where they repeated the same barbarities, and seizing all the arms and ammunition that fell in their way, began to grow formidable to the colony. The Governor no sooner received intimation of this disturbance, than he, by proclamation, subjected the colonists to martial law. All other business was interrupted, and every man took to his arms. The regular troops, joined by the troop of Militia, and a considerable number of volunteers, marched from Spanish Town to St. Mary's, where the insurrection began, and skirmished with the insurgents; but, as they declined standing any regular engagement, and trusted chiefly to bush fighting, the Governor employed against them the free blacks, commonly known by the name of the wild negroes, now peaceably settled under the protection of the Government. These auxiliaries, in consideration of a price set upon the heads of the rebels, attacked them in their own way, slew them by surprise until their strength was broken, and numbers made away with themselves in despair, so that the insurrection was supposed to be quelled about the beginning of May, but in June it broke out again with redoubled fury, and the rebels were reinforced to a very considerable number. The regular troops and the Militia formed a camp, under the command of Colonel Spragge, who sent out detachments against the negroes, a great number of whom were killed and some taken, but the rest, instead of submitting, took shelter in the woods and mountains. The prisoners, being tried and found guilty of rebellion, were put to death by a variety of tortures. Some were hanged, some beheaded, some burned, and some fixed alive upon gibbets.

" The expense of putting down this rebellion was £100,000.

" The revolt of the Maroons in 1795 was not finally extinguished until 1796.

" That of 1832 (exclusive of the value of property destroyed, viz. £1,154,583) cost £161,596, and Parliament was compelled to grant a loan of £500,000 to assist the almost ruined planters. About two hundred were killed in the field, and about five hundred executed."*

At present, £25,000 will cover the outlay of Governor Eyre; but it will be hard to count the cost in blood and treasure, if his Excellency's suspension gives the rebels heart of grace to break out again as they did in 1760.

When we reflect that Jamaica, with a fine climate and a soil sufficiently rich and fertile to sustain with ease three millions of inhabitants, is yet dependent upon imports of provisions for the support of its population, scarcely numbering half a million, the slightest reflection will convince the most confirmed negrophilist, that the day has arrived when legislation, with regard to the labouring population, can be no longer delayed. The negro *must* be made to work; he has been, I am sorry to say, encouraged to look upon liberty as licence, and thirty years of such teaching has vastly prejudiced his advance in civilization, and at the same time ruined his country.

It is my deliberate opinion, 1st, that the widespread discontent amongst the negroes had its birth in the granting unlimited freedom and equality to them before they were taught to understand the responsibilities attached to such privileges.

2nd, that the imagination of the negroes has been inflamed by

* Martin's ' Statistics of the British Colonies.'

the sojourn amougst them of the Haytian* refugees—a black emperor, dukes, counts, generals, and colonels, who kept up quite
an excitement by the expenditure of their ill-gotten wealth,—
naturally making each negro aspire to similar honours.

And, lastly, that this feeling was, however unwittingly, fo-
mented and increased by those persons who, instead of teaching
peace and goodwill towards men; encouraging industry; and
inculcating obedience to law and morality, excited by inflammatory harangues this most excitable people.

The crisis that has arisen, will, it is to be hoped, induce us to
go to the very bottom of this black question, and institute a
careful scrutiny into the merits of the case.

All practical men are united in the belief that the first step
to remedy those evils under which Jamaica groans, is the abolition of the Assembly and constituting the island a Crown Colony.
After this primary step, I would suggest that certain laws should
be enacted, with special reference to the blacks,—a Vagrant Act,
for example,—the sole punishment, banishment.

If the negro is idle and debauched, he should be sent out of
the country; those who are disposed to work should be hired by
contract, for a given term; breach of contract on either side
severely punishable; no penitentiary or prisons as a premium to
negro sloth, but the one punishment—banishment.

I may be asked, how about the cost? I reply, it would be con-
siderably under the present expense of supporting vice in prison.
Hayti, which is within sight of Jamaica, should be selected as
the locality for the future residence of those negroes to whom
the new regulations in Jamaica might prove distasteful.

* The people of Jamaica have a dreadful warning before them in the
fate of Hayti. Compare the proceedings of *les Amis des Noirs*, "the
friends of the blacks" of 1788, with those of the professional philanthropists
of the present day, and say in what they differ. Is the danger of pro-
pagating theories of liberty and equality, less because it is done under the
cloak of religion? I will not enter on a recital of the horrid massacres to
which the mania of the pretended philanthropists of that age gave birth,
and which were only such as may with certainty be expected when ignorant savages are instigated to insurrection, and are able to overwhelm
those in authority over them. But the very sight of that fine island in
its present state, is sufficient to overpower the mind with the most melan-
choly reflections. And to think that by the interference of persons who
have never seen Jamaica, and have no knowledge of the sum of human
happiness they are endangering, it may soon become as desolate as Hayti,
is most painful to contemplate.

The laws of Hayti exclude the whites from any rights whatever, but the country is open to a black man, who becomes a citizen at once; and I have no doubt that the Jamaica blacks leaving their country for their country's good, at a cost of 5s. per head, would be received with open arms by their Haytian brethren. At all events, it is not too much to exact this small return from Hayti. Some well-considered plan of firmly governing the blacks must be *at once* adopted, or the whites will shortly, in self-preservation, be compelled to abandon Jamaica.

I expect the latter alternative, because the principles on which alien and dissimilar races ought to be governed, is not yet understood by our rulers.

Jamaica is not the only proof of this : the state of St. Vincent, Antigua, New Zealand, the Cape of Good Hope, to say nothing of India, attests that "how to govern alien races" has yet to be learnt.

Let us take the negro as we find him, as God designed him, not a white man, nor the equal of a white man. "That he can exist in a community of Anglo-Saxons on terms of political and social equality, is both physically and morally impossible."*

It is astounding to hear those who have never been out of their own country, vehemently laying down the law, in opposition to men who have spent great part of their time in obtaining knowledge and experience in official, professional, or commercial life in the colonies.

That popular periodical, ' Fun,' has lately given an analysis of those gentlemen who have undertaken to legislate for Jamaica,— a China merchant, a dissenting minister, a blind man, a street preacher, and an amiable brewer,—but even such a combination as this will fail.

Who, then, will discover the true art of governing alien races ? I answer, the statesman, who makes anthropological science his study, and the basis of his efforts for improving the condition of mankind.

* " The White Republican " of ' Fraser's Magazine,' [the editor of the ' Cosmopolitan.']

The PRESIDENT then proposed that the thanks of the meeting
be given to Captain Pim for his paper, which proposition was
carried unanimously, and with loud cheers. He said it had been
left to him, as President of the Society, to decide whether the
latter part of the paper should be read, and he thought it best
to submit the question to the meeting. They had decided that
it should be, and had expressed their satisfaction with the paper
altogether. Every one must now be anxious for a full and fair
discussion; but he desired to remind those who intended to
speak, that it should be done with temper and fairness, and that
the Society were only anxious to arrive at the truth. He begged
to introduce a gentleman who had resided in Jamaica for the
last thirty years, and he called on him to address the meeting in
the first instance.

Mr. ARIA rose and said :—I appear before you, Mr. Chairman
and Gentlemen, with great diffidence, being a perfect stranger,
but feel somewhat reassured in speaking on Jamaica matters,
from my long residence there, and intimate acquaintance with
most of the victims of the Morant Bay massacre, as well as
from experience of the affairs of the colony, gained during my
residence there of thirty years. You will permit me to preface
my remarks by observing, that during that long period I never
mixed in the local politics of the place, and hence claim to be
an impartial witness of their effect on the people at large. At
the meetings organized in Kingston, respecting the slave-trade
off the coast of Cuba, I took part in the proceedings, and in
1864 I was the bearer of a memorial, signed for the meeting by
his Lordship the Bishop of Kingston, to the Parliament, and
that memorial was presented to the House of Lords by the
venerable Lord Brougham. I preface my remarks with this
statement, to show that I have endeavoured, with others, to
promote measures tending to benefit the blacks, and I claim to
stand before you to speak of them without the slightest prejudice of colour.

The island of Jamaica is about 160 miles long, by 40 to 50
miles broad, and is divided into three counties, subdivided into
parishes, each presided over by a Custos Rotulorum—an officer
somewhat similar in position to the lords-lieutenant of English
counties. When Dr. Underhill's letter was sent to Governor
Eyre, he naturally referred it to the custodes and magistrates of
the several districts, and reported to the Colonial Office the
result of their information. In a similar way, during the pas
year, the Governor obtained advices that there was great disaf-

fection amongst the negroes. In the month of August, at the requisition of Mr. Custos Salmon, two gunboats were sent to Montego Bay to keep the ill-disposed in check. All this was duly reported to the Colonial Office. Let us now see what the Ministry here did in consequence. Why, they took no notice whatever of the Governor's reports; and although fully aware of the dangerous position of the handful of whites in the colony, nothing was done to strengthen the garrison; on the contrary, the white troops were gradually withdrawn, and the occasional visit of a gunboat was the only naval force under orders of the Commodore at Port Royal.

Now you have heard every person connected with Jamaica complain bitterly of the House of Assembly, and of its influence for evil amongst the negroes. One of the chief causes may be cited in the character of its debates, and the incendiary language indulged in by men like Gordon. You will find in the 'Times' of to-day, several extracts from a letter of the Rev. J. Radcliffe (the highly respected and accomplished Presbyterian minister of Kingston) in proof of this; the style of alluding to the relative relation of the 360,000 blacks, 60,000 coloured, and 12,000 whites, and the threats of rebellion, and of driving the latter into the sea, were indulged in, in presence of a mob of negroes—spectators at the bar of the House. In Jamaica, the public have free admission to these debates, and I remember being present when one of these inflammatory speeches was loudly cheered by the mob, to whom, in fact, it was addressed. Harangues of this kind to Fenians or Chartists, or if adopted here by your Brights, Underhills, Chamerovzows, etc., fall harmless in the face of the majesty of the law and the force of public opinion; the Executive has ever at command the means of crushing any *émeute*. But, my friends, consider the difference in Jamaica: the Government there had not a half-regiment of regular troops, nor a single ship of war, to use at the emergency; hence, you may judge of the need for the greatest promptitude and energy, to quell the revolt and to prevent it spreading in the other parishes; hence the necessity for martial law, and the strongest measures of repression.

People in Jamaica, assuredly the best judges of the gravity of the situation, cannot comprehend why the great English people allow themselves to be led by a small section, hailing from Exeter Hall, who, for party purposes, have published garbled statements, and have attacked the Governor and authorities in the foulest language. Is this the fair play to be expected of Englishmen? Doubtless the opinions expressed by Messrs. Buxton, Potter, Bright, Underhill, and others, are entitled to consideration; are we not to expect the like of the statements and opinions of the men on the spot,—Admiral Hope, Sir Leopold M'Clintock, Colonel

Whitfield, and many other distinguished men ? Mr. Buxton, in
a letter to the 'Standard,' on the 27th ult., says :—" No doubt
Governor Eyre deserves credit for the promptitude with which
he suppressed the insurrection ; in such an 'emergency' people
sitting at ease at home must not criticize matters too closely,"
etc.

Now, I complain that Mr. Buxton will not act in the spirit of
this paragraph, and maintain a reticent course pending the report of the Commission ; but, on the contrary, endeavours to
mislead the public with misstatements, and condemns the military authorities, of whose proceedings he is by no means a com-
petent judge. Mr. Buxton disclaims all connection with the
violent anti-slavery negrophilists ; but he does more mischief in
asserting "the Governor had two regiments of regular troops,
the Buffs from Barbadoes, and a battalion of black troops came
from Nassau." He knew quite well these were sent for after the
outbreak, and that none arrived in Jamaica until it was quelled.
He also speaks of the insurrection being confined to a single
spot, at the east end of the island ; full well knowing that the revolt spread immediately from Morant Bay, on the east, to An-
notto Bay, on the north, a circumference of over forty miles.

With relation to G. W. Gordon, it appears to be the feeling
of every person of respectability and position in the island, that
his speeches and proclamations were the prime cause of the fearful events we have to deplore. What right had he to tell the
negroes the Governor was a bad man, the magistrates unjust
and tyrannical ; that the planters employed Coolies to their prejudice, and paid them double wages, whilst they—the negroes—
starved ; that they ought to have £12 each given to them, and
that they should do as in Hayti (where the blacks and coloured
united to destroy the whites, and ultimately the coloured met
the same fate) ? Such harangues as this, to thousands and thousands of half-civilized, idle negroes, was laying the train which a
spark would ignite ; do you wonder, then, the blacks, confident in
their numbers, took the law in their hands, burnt the Court of
Justice, and murdered the magistrates ? and do you wonder that
the people of Jamaica point out Gordon as the arch-agitator, the
cause of all this frightful mischief?

Much has been said in some of the public press about Gordon
being a man of large property. and an inference drawn that he
could have no motive to agitate against the upper classes in the
colony. Now, the fact is, although Gordon had much land, it
was never paid for : large judgments are recorded against him,
and in November his property was levied on, to satisfy claims
of English creditors. He was in the habit of drawing cheques
on the Jamaica Bank without having funds there. I have
had these dishonoured drafts, and had to instruct clients not

to take them. I believe, at the Manchester meeting, one enthusiastic gentleman claimed Gordon (who never was absent from Jamaica) as a *protégé*, educated there. I wonder, if so, whether he learned this sort of mercantile morality in the Manchester school. Gordon was always considered a troublesome man by his own class. In the House of Assembly a law was passed, limiting the right of each member to speak to twenty minutes, for the purpose of checking his incessant speeches; in 1863, he took a leading part in the so-called religious revivals, and, having quitted the Church of England, opened a Baptist tabernacle on his own account, and under his own regulations. At this period he closed his place of business in Kingston for three days, and posted outside a placard:—"I, G. W. Gordon, in the name of the God of Abraham, Isaac, and Jacob, intend fasting for the sins of the land for three days." People thought he was crazy; the poor negroes became wild with religious frenzy; Ministers of the Established Church, Presbyterians, Moravians, Wesleyans, and others, in vain endeavoured to guide or check these excesses. The orgies and blasphemy at most of these chapel-meetings, like that at Paul Bogle's place after the massacre at Morant Bay, were frightful in the extreme. The negroes kept holiday from six to eight weeks at Christmas, neglecting even their provision grounds; and when the severe drought set in afterwards, numbers of them suffered severely. You can imagine, from all this, the character of Gordon's influence over the people, and the great dread of its ultimate power for evil, felt by all classes of the whites and coloured people.

I have received many letters from various parts of the island, all expressing the greatest indignation at the treatment Governor Eyre has received at the hands of the Ministry here. All persons of respectable position and property concur in expressing the deepest gratitude to Mr. Eyre and the authorities for the able and decided measures they adopted; there is not a shadow of doubt, that if the Governor had hesitated to do his duty for forty-eight hours, the whole island would have been in insurrection; admitting, for argument's sake, there was no organized plan for the revolt, its effect amongst the 360,000 negroes, if successful at Morant Bay, would have been to combine them all to "drive the whites into the sea," as threatened in the House of Assembly. The Governor, in conformity with the whole tenor of his history and antecedents, nobly, ably, and zealously crushed the rebellion; and all who, like myself, have relatives and property in the island, feel that we are indebted to him, under God's providence, for the preservation of both. We think the action of Earl Russell, in degrading Governor Eyre for his noble conduct in the execution of his duty, will leave an eternal stain on the fair fame of that nobleman.

We expect the people of England will nevertheless render justice, imperatively demanded in this matter, and, in Mr. Charles Buxton's words, criticize calmly the proceedings of the colonial authorities at an emergency like this, which no man can appreciate or realize fully, unless present at the time. We think, if there is to be sympathy for Gordon and for a mob of negroes, banded together·to murder and pillage, still more is to be extended to the families of the victims of this tragedy. My Jamaica friends say, at your meetings and in the newspapers before·named, we find much said on behalf of Gordon, but not one word about his victims,—the Baron Kettelholdt, Hire, Price, Hitchings, Cooke, Alberga, and others. They can scarcely believe that any portion of the public press of England to be so influenced by the ranting orators of Exeter Hall. It is just the feeling, Mr. Chairman, that causes us to be so unpopular with the great body of the American people. The constant interference in the institutions of other nations, which this party pursues, gains us an evil report amongst them.

I have heard many Americans attribute the late war, and much of their troubles, to the agitation originating here,—whether rightly or not, I am not prepared to say; but I record what I have frequently heard : " Why don't your anti-slavery people look after your white slaves at home?" say the Americans. "Why not educate your ignorant masses, and alleviate the frightful amount of misery and distress to be seen daily in London, instead of directing their energies in interfering with us and others, thousands of miles from the shores of England ?"

In like manner have the people in Jamaica to complain of the course pursued there by the anti-slavery people. The history of the blacks in Hayti shows they are incapable of self-government, and the necessity that exists for their being under the guidance of a strong executive. I believe, as a Crown colony, with a firm administration, the blacks in Jamaica may yet be materially advanced in the scale of civilization : they are a race easily led for good or for evil. Remove the pernicious influences which have caused the latter, and a better state of things will soon be apparent. If the 10,000 whites are to remain in the colony, surrounded by 360,000 blacks, the former must be placed in a position of security, by a strong Government, and by the proper application of the laws of industry and labour, which naturally regulate all well-managed communities.

I fear, Mr. Chairman, I have trespassed too long on your time, and I will now conclude my remarks, thanking you and the meeting for the honour awarded me in permitting me to address my countrymen on this occasion.

Mr. Hugh R. Semper said :—Sir, feeling the deepest interest
in the question under discussion this evening, in consequence
of possessing an intimate acquaintance with most of the West
Indian Colonies, having for years taken part in the legislation of
more than one island, and having discharged the duties of a
magistrate, and still having the honour to hold the Commission
of the Peace, I trust I may be pardoned for venturing to address
so large and distinguished an audience on a subject that so
vitally concerns the West Indies.

In doing this, I feel that my first duty is to thank Captain
Pim for the able, comprehensive, and truly eloquent lecture,
which he has addressed to us this evening. It evidences not
only great research, acute powers of observation, and marked
ability; but also proves that its author is possessed of that moral
vigour, that chivalrous spirit and fearless determination which
counts no odds when defending the cause of truth and justice, and
which Englishmen, above all things, so much admire, and so
thoroughly appreciate.

In touching upon that part of the question which relates to
the character of the negro, I have only to add that, though utterly
unfitted for self-government, or, as a class, for possessing extensive electoral privileges, my experience, gathered in various
capacities, as a proprietor, as a magistrate, and as an officer
of the Colonial Protective Force, compels me to say that
they often display many good and excellent qualities. They
are capable of strong and earnest attachment to their superiors, and I honestly believe that if it were not for the pernicious influence so fatally exercised upon them by unscrupulous demagogues, by well-intentioned, but rash and enthusiastic philanthropists, but, above all, by those who, with
diabolical hypocrisy, use religion as a cloak to carry out their
levelling principles—to sow those seeds of hatred and disunion
which produce bitter fruit, and so often lead to those terrible
colonial tragedies, such as that recently enacted at Morant Bay,—
I say, Sir, that I honestly believe that if it were not for all
this and that if the negro were not encouraged in vice, indolence,
and outrage, peace, order, and harmony would prevail; and the
black man, as he exists in the West Indies, would develop into
a good, and even an industrious citizen, capable of attaining com-
fort and happiness for himself, and contributing largely to the
prosperity of the land, in which he enjoys a thousand blessings,
and far greater political freedom and higher privileges than are
enjoyed by any labouring class in Europe.

Despite the assertions that are made by men more ready
to traduce than to substantiate their charges, I can fearlessly
challenge them to produce a single statute that gives evidence of
one-sided or class legislation. I can fearlessly challenge them to

prove either that the blacks are oppressed, and the courts of justice closed against them, or that the minds of the judges are warped by improper class prejudices. In addition to the public hospitals, lunatic asylums, the poor-rates, the public schools, which each colony possesses, many of them have a staff of district medical officers, whose duty is to supply, gratuitously, medicine and medical attendance to the labouring population. Large grauts are also constautly being made to enable the health officers to improve the sanitary condition of the negro villages in the different colonies. To do all these things, which are for the exclusive benefits of the "oppressed blacks," the white men,—who, it is said, are the legislators,—voluntarily impose heavy taxes upon their landed property, and upon the exported product of that property.

Not many years ago, the island of St. Kitt's was afflicted with that terrible scourge, cholera, which swept off a fourth of the black population. The disease was almost entirely confined to the blacks, and yet the local government did not for a moment hesitate as to the course it should adopt. Numerous hospitals were established, every medical man was employed, a large staff of house-to-house visitors were retained, and relief in every shape was extended to the unfortunate sufferers. The result was, that the island had to expend the large sum of fifty thousand dollars; and as its ordinary resources became exhausted, a special tax had to be levied to meet the deficiency. This tax, I need hardly add, for the most part fell upon the properties of those whose kindness and humanity were not restrained because negroes were its recipients.

That there has been suffering among the labouring classes in Jamaica, is unquestionable; but to whom, or to what, I ask, is this suffering attributable? Certainly not to the planter. It is in the first place the result of two severe seasons of drought, and of the low price of sugar. The negroes having refused (notwithstanding the heavy premiums that were offered) to enter into a contract of service with the planters, the latter have in many instances been driven to introduce foreign labour at a heavy cost to themselves. These contract labourers the planters are compelled to keep in employment during the severest seasons, as long as the contract exists; the negroes would have enjoyed a similar protection if they had chosen to enter into an agreement, neither more nor less stringent in its terms than those that are so constantly made in the agricultural districts in this country. Surely there exists no moral or legal reason why the planter should be called upon to incur considerable loss by giving employment to labourers whom he does not require, simply because distress prevails.

Let me ask, did Mr. Bright and other mill-owners continue

to employ their operatives when the high price of cotton rendered the continued employment of such operatives unprofitable?

It was well said, Sir, of Robespierre, by a celebrated French author, that he certainly appeared to love liberty, for he not only took care to enjoy his own, but he sought to possess that of others also. In the present case, the reckless accusers of the colonists, not only demand a full share of freedom for the blacks, but seek "*per fas et nefas*" to deprive the whites of every vestige of it.

I am aware that amongst the persons who have raised their voice against Governor Eyre, and those who acted under his authority, there are many men whose generosity of purpose and nobleness of character we all admire; and I can only therefore deplore that under false impressions, created by grossly exaggerated accounts of the extent of retributive punishment, they should have fallen into fellowship with a party who seek to mislead the public mind of this country by such infamous statements as "eight miles of dead," "thousands killed," and other utterly false accounts regarding Gordon's trial, put forward by renegade reporters and such-like.

Before taking my seat, I must earnestly crave your indulgence and the indulgence of my audience for a few moments longer, while I say a few words on Gordon's trial. It would be impossible, Sir, on an occasion like this, to notice the many theories that have been started, or the many terrible threats that have been so menacingly uttered. I will therefore only allude to the opinion recently given to the Jamaica committee by two eminent lawyers, Mr. Fitzjames Stephen and Mr. James, the Attorney-general of the Duchy of Lancaster. These gentlemen tell us that the Governor of Jamaica had only the common law right, which the Crown possesses in this country, to repel force by force, even to the destruction of life and property; but deny his right to appoint courts-martial to sit in judgment, except while there was active resistance to the law. In this country, the Crown, as late as the time of Charles I., exercised the prerogative of creating courts, under what was termed the "law martial." This exercise of the prerogative has been finally destroyed in England by the Bill of Rights; and before martial law could, in consequence of internal disturbance, be proclaimed here, both Houses must join in suspending the operation of the Habeas Corpus Act. The 96th sect. 9th Vict. c. 30, expressly authorizes, by the "opinion and advice of a council of war, the proclamation of martial law, limiting, however, the period of its existence to *thirty* days, unless expressly continued by the advice of a council of war as aforesaid." The succeeding declaration also authorizes the Governor, with such advice as aforesaid, to limit the operation of martial law to particular districts.

I contend that this special prerogative of proclaiming martial law and of constituting courts-martial in times of disturbance, still exists in Jamaica, apart from any preceding legislative action. " It is absurd," says Lord Mansfield, in the celebrated case of *Campbell* v. *Hall*, " to suppose that in the colonies they should carry all the laws of England with them; they carry only such as are applicable to their situation. I remember it has been determined in the Council; there was a question whether the Statute of Charitable Uses operated on the island of Nevis; it was determined it did not; and no laws, except such as were applicable to their condition, unless expressly enacted." It is clear that this peculiar privilege of personal liberty was not considered applicable to the condition of a young colony, or a necessary incident of colonization; for I find in Second 'Chalmers' Opinions,' p. 69, an eminent lawyer, the Solicitor-General of George II., thus advising the Crown respecting an Act passed by one of the Colonial Legislatures :—" This law likewise enacts that all laws in force in England relating to personal liberty and to property, shall be in force in those islands, which I conceive to be very improper." Acting on this opinion, the Crown disallowed the Bill. I have searched in vain, Sir, through the statute book of Jamaica for any evidence to show that legislation has deprived the Crown of this special prerogative; while, on the other hand, I have further found, in First 'Chalmers' Opinions,' p. 233, these forcible words :—" The prerogative, unless where it is abridged by grants, etc., made to the respective provinces, is that power over the subjects which, by the common law of the land, abstracted from all Acts of Parliament, and grants and liberties, the King could rightfully exercise in England." The Crown, in Jamaica, I submit, then, clearly possesses the prerogatives which it from time to time exercised in this country up to the time of the passing of the Bill of Rights. If these views are correct, it then follows that in Jamaica the Executive not only possesses the common law right to repel force by force, but that the Governor, as the representative of the Sovereign, was warranted in proclaiming martial law without any legislative action, and that courts-martial can sit as legally constituted courts in a disturbed district. I fully admit that the case of *Fabrigas* v. *Mostyn*, quoted by the learned counsel, conclusively establishes the principle that a Governor can be rendered liable in this country for an illegal act committed abroad. In this case Governor Mostyn had heavy damages given against him, because he acted in diametrical opposition to all laws ; but the learned counsel had not the candour to mention at the same time, to those who sought their opinion, that the case of *Dutton* v. *Howell*, mentioned in *Fabrigas* v. *Mostyn*, also established another principle, namely, that a Governor could plead as a bar to any action or indictment, the laws of the colony under which he acted; or, to give the following words of Lord Mansfield, used when giving final judgment against Governor Mostyn :— Justice Powell says, in the case of *Way* v. *Yally*, that an action "of false imprisonment had been brought here against the Governor of Jamaica for the imprisonment there, and the laws of the courts were given in evidence;" and, adds Lord Mansfield, "he showed, I suppose, by the laws of the country, an Act which justified that imprisonment, and the court received it, to be sure, as they ought to do. Whatever is a justification in the place where the thing is done, ought to be a justification in the place where the thing is tried." Governor Mostyn was punished because he could neither plead that he had properly exercised the prerogative of the Crown, or was protected by any local law, or by any *ex post facto* legislation. Governor Eyre, on the contrary, can claim all three. There is nothing illegal in proclaiming martial law : the constitution of this country allows it, but only requires preceding legislation; the constitution of Jamaica enables the executive to dispense with such legislation. In any case, it cannot, with a shadow of reason, be denied that the law of Jamaica authorized a warrant being issued against Gordon, and that, whether or not the Governor had the right to proclaim martial law and to create courts-martial, he stands by the subsequent act of the island—the Bill of Indemnity—in precisely the same position as if he had.

The argument used, that as Governor Eyre's consent was required to the Act, he could not pardon himself, shows that the learned gentlemen are really driven to their wits' end to find the slightest shadow of reason to support the earnest desire of a party to prosecute Governor Eyre in this country. An assent has been given to the Bill of Indemnity, not by Edward Eyre, but by the representative of the Sovereign; and if the private individual, Edward Eyre, be subsequently dealt with, he can surely, in all reason and justice, be protected by what is an ample protection for every other British citizen in Jamaica. For instance, is it because a Governor assents to a Bill granting him a salary, as many Governors were formerly in the habit of doing, that therefore he cannot use such salary so granted?

If the learned Counsel's argument on this point be admitted, see what it inevitably leads to. Every felon in Jamaica, every person who has ever been punished in that island, by the authority of the Executive carrying out any law, to which, as Governor, Mr. Eyre had given his consent, could prosecute him in this country, and he would be estopped from pleading that he acted according to the law, because, in his official capacity, he had given the assent of the Crown to that law. The proposition is as monstrous as it is untenable.

Another argument, put forward with great speciousness is

this : That Governor Eyre, if he has committed any crime at all, has committed a crime against the law of this country, and that the Legislature of Jamaica have no authority to pass a Bill of Indemnity, virtually pardoning an offence against the laws of England. It is very true that no colony has a right, in its legislative capacity, to control an Act of the Imperial Parliament; but though the 9th sect. 24 & 25 Vict. c. 100, and the earlier statutes mentioned by the learned counsel, authorize the courts of law in this country to deal with crimes committed by British subjects, either in foreign lands or in any part of Her Majesty's dominions, yet not one of the statutes attempt to give an exclusive jurisdiction to the English courts. They only possess a concurrent jurisdiction with the colonial courts, as the following words of the 9th section of the statute above quoted satisfactorily prove :—

" Provided that nothing herein contained shall prevent any person from being tried in any place out of *England* or *Ireland*, for any murder or manslaughter committed out of England or Ireland, in which such death, stroke, poisoning, or hurt shall happen in the same manner as such person might have been tried before the passing of this Act."

It is evident that the statutes which apply to this question have not established, and that it was not the intention of the English legislature to establish, anything that could in the slightest degree interfere with that principle so clearly laid down by Lord Mansfield, that a Governor, though tried in an English court, and for an alleged breach of English law, can always plead as a bar to any action or indictment, the law of the land under which he acted, and in which the offence charged was committed.

With reference, Sir, to the treatment that Governor Eyre has lately received at the hands of Her Majesty's Government, I hardly dare trust myself to speak on the subject, lest I be tempted to exceed the bounds of temperate discussion. I dread to think what may be the probable consequences of this unjust and impolitic action of the Government. Even if it does not cause all order and authority to be trampled upon in the West Indies,—even if devastation, carnage, and worse than death be not carried into the homestead of every white family, it cannot fail to paralyse the energies of every public servant entrusted with the maintenance of British rule in various quarters of the globe. In saying this, let it not be understood that the friends of the colonies,—that the friends of Governor Eyre,—that the friends of the hapless beings who were so cruelly and treacherously murdered at Morant Bay, shrink from inquiry. They simply demand justice, and that there should be a proper vindication of outraged laws; and I venture to ask this audience, to ask the people of England, not to form, upon grossly exaggerated or wilfully false statements, hasty conclusions.

We are expressly warned by the 'Jamaica Standard' not to place reliance on the notes of Gordon's trial that were stolen from its office; but even on that evidence, imperfect as it doubtless is, there can be no moral doubt of Gordon's guilt. Read his speeches, read his addresses, read his letters, hear what he is proved to have said in Bogle's chapel, and then, I ask, where is there room for doubt? I admit that it might not have been sufficient to legally prove him guilty in a court of law, with numerous legal technicalities governing the reception of evidence; but a court-martial is bound by no such technicalities, and its members, as men of honour and integrity, are simply bound, when sitting, as the court sat at Morant Bay, to declare whether, upon the evidence that has been brought before them (be that evidence what it may), they believe the accused guilty or not guilty.

In dealing equal-handed justice, the Imperial Government should have taken care that no outside pressure induced them to cast censure directly or indirectly upon a man who, they have already testified, in a position of great difficulty and danger, nobly performed his duty, and, at all hazards to himself and to his future career, upheld the menaced authority of his Sovereign.

Judge HIBBERT (of the United States) considered the negro to be naturally capable of civilization, and that under favourable influences the people of Africa might, after a few centuries, be found as civilized as the white races. The condition of a slave was peculiarly unfavourable to moral improvement, for slaves had nothing to care for; but if they gave the negro education, and the same kind of encouragement that was given to the children of white men, they would be equal to them. The negroes were generally admitted to be very "smart" in making a bargain, and he did not think they were in other respects intellectually inferior. Civilization, he said, was quite distinct from religion; for if religion were considered to be an indication of civilization, the African negroes were the highest type of civilization, for they believed more than any other people on the face of the earth—they believed much more than Christians. Civilization, he (Judge Hibbert) contended, consisted in the knowledge men had of their own rights, and a respect for the rights of others; and until we civilized ourselves, we could not expect to do much towards civilizing Africa. America had given the franchise to the negro, and would give them an equal position to the white man. In some of the American states, where the negroes had been free for many years, they had turned out the finest black babies in the world. One thing the negro had to contend against, was the prejudice of the white race, who had a great contempt for them. He never, in his life, saw a white man take off his hat to a negro. Unless they got rid of their prejudices against the blacks, education alone would be of little use: for as long as the negroes had no incitement to improve themselves, they would not be civilized. He believed that the negro is as capable of attaining the highest degree of civilization as the white man; and it should be borne in mind that not many years ago the people of this country were barbarous savages.

Mr. WINWOOD READE said, that he had had more experience of the savage than of the semi-civilized or missionarized negro. He would, however, make a remark on native wars, which might, to some extent, bear upon the subject of the discussion. He had gone up the Gambia with a diplomatic expedition, and had observed that the English had no influence in that river, and were despised by the natives. In the Senegal, which he afterwards ascended, he had found that the French were feared and respected. The reason of this was, that in the late Badaboo war the English had shown great indulgence to their enemies, while the French had always acted upon the contrary principle. Now savages never believe in the existence of those virtues which they do not themselves possess. We spared them from benevolence; they supposed that it was from fear. What he had always said about native wars was this—Avoid them as long as you can; but if you must fight with natives, kill them down. Kill them down not only for self-protection, but from a philanthropic principle. It seems paradoxical to say so, but there may be mercy in a massacre. If the natives had been more sternly dealt with, we should not now have them fixing the precise date when they would take Bathurst, and about to drag us into a war which will probably involve a serious loss of life; he might add, that had not Governor Eyre shown such prompt severity, we should now be sending out troops to save white men's lives, instead of a Commission to sit upon black men's carcases.

Mr. HARRIS said:—With reference to the remarks we have been favoured with by Captain Pim, on the condition of the natives in the interior of Africa, there can be no doubt that, as the traveller recedes from the coast, the more intelligent the inhabitants are, that he meets with.

The pure negro is amalgamated with the more enlightened people of the interior, until they are nearly lost in the great tribe of Foulahs or Foutahs, who, with their numerous and powerful offshoots of Manding, Boondu, Suleimah, Bambarrahs, Serawoolys, and Segos are always to be met within two hundred miles of the coast.

These people possess the leading political and religious power wherever met, are keen traders, and acquire most of the material wealth of the district; they are strict Moslems, and teach the negroes they settle amongst sufficient of their faith to make them feared and respected. They have a literature of their own, and are looked up to by the negro as "bookmen," or superiors. They are easily distinguished from the negro by their regular and prominent features, resembling in their physique the Arab and Moor, to whom they bear a strong affinity.

From personal observation amongst the different negro tribes I have been amongst, with regard to the ideas they have of worshipping a deity, it is not to pray for benefits here or hereafter, but always to be protected from present injury and bodily suffering, the superior object of their worship being the incarnation and ruling power of all evil, nothing of good.

As far as agriculture is concerned, the negro is a tiller of the soil from necessity, but never attempts any improvements, changes, or extensions upon the system handed down to him by his forefathers; and from his natural indolence, all efforts made by philanthropists to induce them to use our common implements of husbandry, or to alter their mode of planting, have been useless.

The negro limits his husbandry to the satisfaction of his daily wants, to procure the support of which, in the tropics, and with a virgin soil, requires but little effort or exertion on their part.

I can support Captain Pim's statement, that the Maroons are pure negroes, from personal observations made amongst the Maroons of Sierra Leone. They were originally freed slaves of Cuba and Jamaica, and were numerous between 1735 and 1745, at which latter date, having attracted the attention of the Jamaica Government by their increasing numbers, they were located in the Blue Mountain Ridges.

The appellation "Maroon" was given to them by the white men, as indicating the freed blacks. In 1784, they numbered 1400 fighting men, and revolted against the British Government in June, 1785,—keeping up for many years a sort of guerilla warfare, and not being finally subdued until March, 1796, and then principally by the use of Cuban bloodhounds. Until this day it is a common term of reproach against the descendants at Sierra Leone, that they were subdued by dogs. The Maroons are principally descendants of the Gold Coast tribes, and still retain amongst them the same religious superstitions, customs, and common names, as, for instance, the naming of their children after the days of the week upon which they are born, such as Quamin (Monday), the son of Quacco (Thursday), each day being denoted by the masculine and feminine gender. They boast of being directly descended, or having been concerned in the Jamaica rebellion at the end of the eighteenth century, as partisans of King Cudjoe, their leader.

Notwithstanding the length of time that has elapsed since the deportation of a portion of these people to Sierra Leone, where they have been absolutely free and unfettered, they look back with pride to the time when they were able to contend with the white man, showing, in my opinion, another instance of their antagonistic feeling to their best benefactors.

Whether the recent outbreak in Jamaica can, in any degree, be traced to these antagonistics of race is worthy our most careful consideration, more particularly with regard to the future government of the negro.

Mr. HENRY LIGGINS said :—When a few hours ago I heard that Captain Bedford Pim, R.N., was to read a paper this evening to the members and friends of this Society, I felt that the subject of the negro would be dealt with in a manner intelligent, plain, and practical, just and truthful, and with that simple telling eloquence, for which the published writings of this highly gifted naval officer have made him conspicuous. I felt it right to come here to confirm the statements I expected him to make ; and I venture to think that I understand the subject, having visited the United States of America, and paid many visits to the West Indies during the last thirty years, and have had opportunities of observing the negro character in sixteen of the islands, British and foreign. During this long period I have had many proofs of devotion, affection, and kindness from the blacks ; as a large employer of labour in the cultivation of sugar estates, I have done my best to improve them in their social condition ; my inclination as well as my worldly interest has always been in their favour, and I could wish that it were not in my power to confirm the accuracy of the views expressed at such length in the able paper that we have all listened to with so much edification ; but I confess that I am bitterly disappointed in all the efforts I have seen made to improve their condition. This is not caused from any lack of schooling given them in their youth, nor from any visible want of mental capacity, for they are ready enough at learning, and have at their fingers' ends the height of the Himalaya mountains, the distance of the earth from the moon, and all such matters as are unsuited to the hands that toil, while they seem to be too proud to learn anything that would be practically useful in everyday life. There is a great inconsistency in their character : they are endowed with capacity to learn anything they please, but I never knew a case where the energy and determination came forth to induce them to apply their knowledge for their own gain in life or for the benefit of their employer

F

From the grandiloquent phraseology of the words they use, you would be inclined to give them credit for a desire to rise to the higher ranks of civilized life; but I have no recollection of ever observing an individual endeavour to advance his position above that station in which it has pleased God to call him. Who ever knew of a black man rising to the position of a gentleman? Now such instances are common enough among the whites all over the world; and the charity schools of this very parish can testify to the fact that many of their humble scholars, who certainly do not receive as advanced an education as the majority of negroes in the West India islands, rising to wealth, honour, and elevated position, the fruit of a well-directed mind and persevering industry.

We observe among the Chinese and the Coolies from India, as well as among the Portuguese from Madeira and the Cape de Verde Islands, who emigrate to the West Indies, a strong desire to work hard, save money, and with their savings become shopkeepers, in which many of them amass considerable fortunes, and ultimately become merchants and the owners of vessels. Several cases of such success have come under my own notice, while the indolent negro looks on in wonder at the rapid strides and comforts of life enjoyed by strangers who have been only a few years among them.

Idleness is the curse of the negro. The men, as a rule, never work if necessity does not compel them to do so; and the women and children do all the drudgery, while the upright, nobly-formed figure of the black man prefers to lie and smoke all day under the shade of a tree, and returning to his hut with savage cruelty and harsh severity towards those whom he ought to love. The horrid cruelty of the blacks, and their neglect of their children, is truly painful to behold, and I think, coupled with their apparently unalterable licentiousness, prove them to be incapable of becoming, under any known conditions, good citizens; and I much fear that we must form the conclusion that the negro is destined to become extinct, if at any time he should lose the protecting care of the white man.

At this late hour I can only occupy the time of this large meeting with a few words on the recent events that have occurred in Jamaica. Nothing has astonished me more than to find that any section of my countrymen should venture to express so strong an opinion as they have done upon a subject about which they must be very imperfectly informed; and I think, as it is impossible that they can enter into the feelings, dreads, and anxieties of the whites of Jamaica, 5000 miles distance, who number only one-fortieth in number with the blacks, that they should rather place themselves in the same dangerous position, and ask themselves if they think they would have acted differently, when they found the upper classes, their daily associates, their neighbours and friends, being brutally murdered around them, their houses sacked and burned, and their plantations laid waste, with their cattle turned loose in the woods; and all this horrid devilry occurring, not because the blacks had any real grievance, for their friends have not pointed out any justly existing cause for dissatisfaction, but because they were known to have been set on by political demagogues, whose treason was well known to all classes in that magnificent colony.

When the intelligence of this rebellion reached this country, all classes were alarmed at the events that had taken place; and it may be assumed that Her Majesty's Government were better informed than individuals. What did they do? Why, the Prime Minister of England and his associates, through the Secretary of State for the Colonies, sent a despatch to Governor Eyre, thanking him and the civil authorities; and the naval and military forces, for the promptitude, energy, and skill displayed by them, in timely crushing out a formidable rebellion, and thus stopping the further sacrifice of property and innocent lives: thereby retaining, I trust, for future usefulness, this bright gem of the British Crown.

Can anything be more depressing to all right-minded men? Can anything be more humiliating to us, from the ridicule with which we shall be assailed by all foreign countries, when it is discovered that our Prime Minister has yielded to the unscrupulous clamour of a section of the lowest class of Baptist ministers, advanced radicals, and political reformers, backed by the worn-out remnant of the Anti-Slavery Society, aided by the 'Star' newspaper, which is so ably conducted, as a rule, that it merits the most severe censure for taking a part so thoroughly un-English as to condemn untried men, the representatives of the Sovereign, whose conduct under most trying circumstances has been approved by all the legal functionaries, the great body of the magistracy, the clergy of all denominations who hold any position for good among the educated classes, and every section of politicians, the merchants, and the whole body of the whites in Jamaica, and last, though not of less importance, by all the proprietors resident in this country who have property in the island, the great mass of the educated people in this country, and Her Majesty's Government?

Governor Eyre has been harshly treated by those who should have upheld him; but I have no doubt that his honest, upright conduct through life, his great ability and aptitude for the duties of his high position, will enable him to pass through the present trial with honour, and I hope that he may be spared to receive the reward that his noble conduct deserves.

I hold in my hand a letter I received the day before yesterday, by the last West Indian mail, written in another island, dated 12th January. The writer, a gentleman of high position, who has himself received special marks of favour from our beloved Queen, writes:—

"In respect to Gordon's execution, what will be said when his father's letter is quoted, stating that he deserved his fate? And this judgment is said to have been given by a man seventy-five years of age.

"Again, there is a lady here who asked, 'How could Gordon say that he did not know Paul Bogle? when I can state that he was his body-servant for years.'

"If Earl Russell sacrifices a Governor to appease popular clamour, then who will be found to put down rebellion in Her Majesty's colonies without fearing he goes to duty with a rope round his neck?"

Does that active-minded Secretary of the Anti-Slavery Society really believe that "his dear friend Gordon" was penning the truth when he wrote that Governor Eyre purloined public money, and with it bought a pianoforte for his own family, and smuggled it through the custom-house?

It is well understood that it is the custom for Governors to be allowed their personal effects to pass through the customs without the payment of duties; and Gordon knew this as well as any one in Jamaica, and must be branded for writing a deliberate lie with a view to deceive the people of England.

It is quite the fashion among some classes of religious fanatics in this country to approve of everything done by the negro; to make a pet of him, and at the same time to censure the deeds of the whites, whether right or wrong; and I regret to notice that in the last two numbers of the 'Cotton Supply Association Reporter,' of Manchester, there are articles censuring an Act recently passed in Antigua, and approved by the Colonial Office, to punish offenders for stealing cotton, which Act was found necessary to protect the fields of the whites from being robbed.

From the means I have had of observation, I am satisfied that the greatest misfortune of the negro is the interference of the Anti-Slavery Society and the teaching of Baptist and other religious sects, whose whole aim is directed to unsettle his mind, make him dissatisfied with his lot, and urge him to extort from his master wages that his profits do not enable him to give. This is well known to be the cause of the present ruin, that, like a dark cloud, hangs over Jamaica.

Indolence is the cause of all the vice of the negro; and if his real friends would take my advice, and urge him to habits of steady continuous work for six days a week, for the fair wages which the planter would then be able to afford, they would make him a useful being, and our West Indian Colonies would again add largely to the wealth of the mother-country; and his soul would be spared from the desire for treason and murder, and we should not again hear of impious oaths and glorious congratulations over foul murders and horrible mutilations, and drunken orgies in Baptist meeting-houses.

Gentlemen, I think our sympathy should be with the murdered whites and their disconsolate families and desolate homes, and not, as the Anti-Slavery Society would desire, with the murderous blacks, who met summary vengeance from the soldiers of their own colour.

I think we ought to thank our stars that we have a Governor, and officers of the navy and army, who so fearlessly upheld the honour and dignity of our country; and I think we ought to unite in thanking God that those efforts were crowned with success, and, under Providence, the murder of all the whites was prevented, and the colony of Jamaica, second to no place in the world for beauty and fertility, is still preserved to the British Crown.

(The speaker was frequently interrupted with applause, and resumed his seat amid loud cheers.)

Dr. SEEMANN, V.P., said:—When, twenty years ago, I left Europe I held very much the same opinions about the negro as most of those do who know him from second-hand sources only. I thought him deserving of pity, and requiring only to be put to school, and in the full possession of freedom, to become equal, if not superior, to the white man. I would scarcely believe myself that 1 once held these absurd opinions, if I did not find them recorded in my own handwriting. I had not been long in the West Indies before facts proved stronger than my theory. I saw the negro in the full enjoyment of all the privileges of a British subject, with plenty of profitable labour before him, and yet not availing himself of these chances, and ruining some of the finest colonies in the world by his indolence. Afterwards I had still better opportunities of studying him in the Spanish American Republics; and when, after a voyage round the world of seven years' duration, I returned once more to England, I had entirely abandoned the ideas with which I set out. All my subsequent experience, in every part of the world, confirmed my conviction that the equality of the negro and the white man, and the possibility of elevating the negro to the standard of the white by education, are mere delusions of the half-informed.

I am far from underrating the power of those who advocate the equality of the negro with ourselves. Late events have proved it. Everybody who has travelled in the United States must have observed the ill-disguised contempt with which the majority of Northerners regard the negro. Yet so perfect was the organization of the abolitionists, and so clever were their tactics, that the North could be made to fight the South and make the rights of the negroes one of their battle-cries! Too late the Americans discovered by whom they were led by the nose, and that the anthropological theory, for the vindication of which some of their best blood was spilt, was rotten at the core.

It is singular that the advocates of negro equality and fraternity do not make a practical application of their theory to themselves. Why don't they persuade their sons and daughters to intermarry with negroes? I am sure they would not maintain that doctrine for a moment, if called upon thus to prove the sincerity of their convictions. A refined white man cannot be in the company of negroes without feeling disgusted by the abominable smell emanating from them. By special pleading you may get over many of the objections preferred against the negro. You may argue away his ugliness, by declaring that, as there is no accounting for taste, you see nothing but lines of beauty in him; you may excuse his indolence by pointing to heaps of idlers amongst ourselves; his cruelty, by quoting the history of Nero and other monsters; his ignorance, by the thousands of dupes and fools in the very centres of civilization; but how will you get over the repulsive odour peculiar to the black skin, and particularly nauseous on a hot tropical day? With this obstacle in the way, can there be any real intimacy between the negro and the white? Or where there is, can it be called any other name but degradation on the part of the Europeans?

Anthropologists have still so many grave questions to solve, that they might be fairly excused for postponing the discussion on the negro's equality with, or inferiority to, the white man. But it is their duty to speak out when the advocates of equality act in a way which must lead to the total extinction of the white race in tropical America. In the tropics the white man labours under so many disadvantages from the climate, that he can only exist there in the position of master. Even then he must recruit his family by constant infusion of fresh blood from home, or else doom it to extinction. The negro, on the contrary, suffers from no climatic disadvantages: he can perform field and other heavy work without suffering in health, and he does not require an infusion of fresh blood to make him thrive and multiply. The two races are thus placed in a position which gives a preponderating advantage to the negro. There is only one thing in the white man's favour—his intellect; and this sole advantage is neutralized by those who insist on the negro's intellect being of equal calibre. In the British West Indies the negroes have not been able to carry out this theory of equality to its legitimate results. But in Hayti and several of the Spanish American Republics they have already done so. There have been in those countries innumerable insurrections, of which the late Jamaica one is but a faint copy; and in every instance they have been directed against the whites. Every fresh rising brings the black element more to the surface. In some places a white face is now as rarely seen as a black in London. Anarchy, such as the world has seldom beheld, is the normal state of things. Bolivar, the liberator of Columbia, foresaw all this. Every word of the remarkable speech he made a few days before his death, has come true. He took so desponding a view of the future of those countries, that he advised all sensible men to emigrate. "If it were possible," he concludes, "that a part of the world could relapse into chaos, it would be Spanish America."

The PRESIDENT then called on Commander Bedford Pim to reply to the remarks of the various speakers. He said that the Society was much indebted to Commander Pim for coming boldly forward to read a paper on this most important subject, and he was proud to find the gallant officer's lengthened experience had led him to entertain similar views to those expressed at the Anthropological Society three years ago.

Commander BEDFORD PIM begged to return his sincere thanks for the manner in which his paper had been listened to; he had felt a glow of delight at the enthusiastic reception accorded by a crowded and highly respectable audience, to the common-sense view of the black question, which he had had the honour to lay before them; and he had been especially delighted at the strong feeling, so warmly evinced, in condemning the conduct of the Government in this matter; for whether Governor Eyre was right or wrong, it was quite clear that a rowdy invasion of Downing Street ought not to have been tolerated for one moment by ministers having the slightest regard, not for their own, but the nation's dignity.

Besides, the Government of this great country ought to have been sufficiently self-reliant to have taken the case into their own hands, and at least to have given Governor Eyre the opportunity of vindicating his conduct before superseding him.

Practical men were united in their condemnation of the "deposition and degradation" of Governor Eyre, not only from a feeling of contempt at witnessing the abandonment of a tried and faithful public servant, but because a more ill-judged and hazardous measure could hardly have been adopted in the face of recent events,—such a measure as neither Wellington nor Palmerston would ever have assented to.

He trusted that any incompleteness in his paper would be forgiven, as other avocations of an engrossing nature had occupied him during its preparation; but he felt so keenly on the subject, that he had waived all personal considerations, in the strong sense of duty which impelled him to bring the matter forward.

In conclusion, he earnestly hoped that if ever he should find himself in a similar position to that of Governor Eyre, he might have the courage, determination, and self-reliance to act precisely as his Excellency had done.

As soon as the President left the chair, three cheers for Governor Eyre were loudly called for, and responded to most enthusiastically, after which the meeting separated at a late hour.

THE END.

R.

J. E. TAYLOR AND CO., PRINTERS,
LITTLE QUEEN STREET, LINCOLN'S INN FIELDS.

www.ingramcontent.com/pod-product-compliance
Lightning Source LLC
Chambersburg PA
CBHW020225090426
42735CB00010B/1594